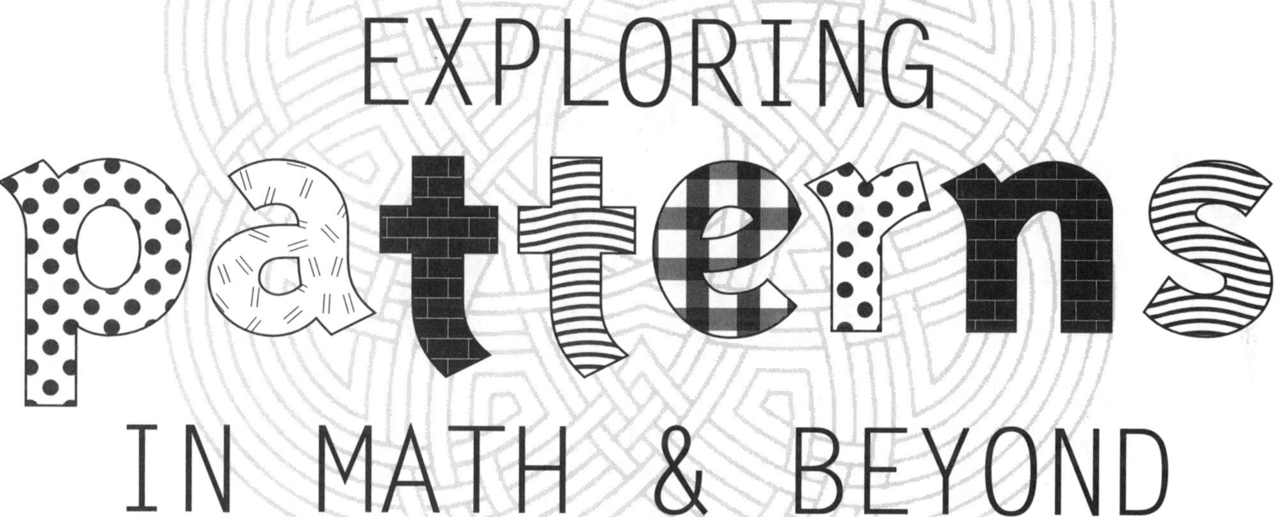

EXPLORING patterns IN MATH & BEYOND

30 Easy, Playful & Creative Patterning Activities
That Teach Across the Curriculum

by Betsy Franco

SCHOLASTIC
PROFESSIONAL BOOKS

New York • Toronto • London • Auckland • Sydney • Mexico City • New Dehli • Hong Kong

dedication

For Tali and her children

Special thanks to Ben, Etai, Jamie, Jenny, José, Kyo, Mailee, Maya, Melissa, Mia, Michael, Nidia, Noa, Sebi, Spencer, and the children in Denise's class, for helping me with each and every activity.

Thank you to the following teachers at El Carmelo School: Denise Dauler, Karen Lemoine, Diane McCoy, and Peri Baloun.

Edited by
Karen Kellaher

Cover design by
Norma Ortiz

Interior design and illustration by
Holly Grundon

Interior photos courtesy of
Betsy Franco

ISBN: 0-590-64405-X

Table of contents

Note to the Teacher

Defining the Word

People of all ages nod their heads when the word *pattern* is mentioned. But what does it really mean? What are the ingredients of a pattern?

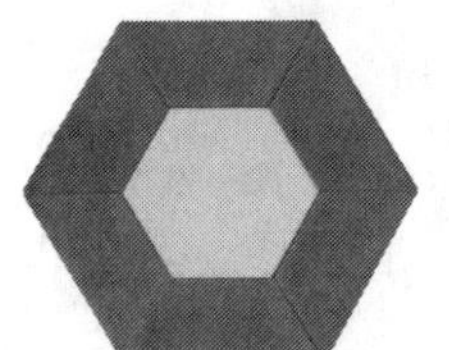

A kindergartner said,

"A pattern is like a color, a color, a color, but different colors in between."

A first grader said,

"A pattern is when something goes right after the other and keeps going the same way."

A second grader said,

"A pattern is something that goes over and over again."

A seventh grader said,

"A pattern is a combination of something—a set of colors, numbers, or shapes—that repeats itself."

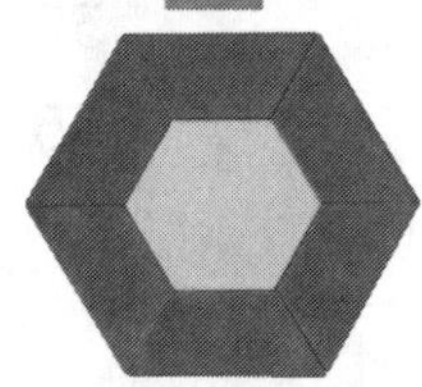

A math major said,

"A pattern has a rule that lets you extend it indefinitely."

A teacher said,

"A pattern is something that has a repeated format."

A quilter said,

"A pattern is an organization of colors and shapes that come together in harmony."

The wonderful thing about patterns is that all of these definitions are correct!

Note to the Teacher

Why are **patterns** important in learning?

Patterns are not only beautiful and fun. They are the basis for important thinking and reasoning skills in the early years and beyond. The benefits of teaching patterns are substantial:

- Children learn to look for patterns when involved in problem-solving situations.
- Children who understand patterns have a solid foundation for learning math concepts.
- Children make connections when given a set of numbers or a set of data on a graph.
- Children see patterns in poetry and literature.
- Children sense order in the universe.
- Children are more aware of symmetry and other geometric patterns.
- Children are more likely to notice patterns in science experiments.
- Children develop a sense of rhythm with regard to sound and movement.
- Children begin to appreciate the beauty, rhythm, and cycles of nature (visual and auditory).

How can **children** work with patterns?

Children can see patterns, hear patterns, create patterns, and break patterns. They can continue patterns, vary patterns, and predict patterns. They can fill in the gaps in patterns and find the repeating elements in patterns. They can figure out if a pattern exists in a particular situation. And they can use patterns to solve problems.

Where do patterns fit in the **curriculum?**

Patterns certainly play an important part in mathematical thinking and problem solving. But why stop there? Fascinating patterns can also be found in other areas of the curriculum. Think about science and the symmetrical patterns of a butterfly wing or a six-sided snowflake. Consider the artistic patterns in beaded jewelry and fabric designs. Notice patterns in music and on the calendar. Appreciate the special patterns in language arts which are found in poetry, cumulative stories, and predictable picture books. Pattern is a theme that runs throughout the curriculum—unifying, organizing, and bringing concepts into sharper focus.

How to use **this book**

This book was designed to be easy for you to use no matter how you structure your teaching. You may want to focus on patterns as your theme of the month. Or you may decide to choose one pattern activity per week. For your convenience, the activities are grouped by main curriculum area. Of course, most of the activities have applications across several curriculum areas. To identify these cross-curricular connections, see the matrix on page 6.

Curriculum Matrix

	math	art	science	sound & movement	language arts	multi-cultural/ social studies
What Is a Pattern?, p.7	●	●	●	●	●	
Patterns to See and Hear, p.9		●	●	●		
Shrinking Shapes, p.11	●	●				
Calendar Patterns, p.14	●	●			●	
Even-Odd Architects, p.16	●					
Even Plus Even, p.18	●					
Tiles to Hamster Cages, p.19	●	●				
Marvelous Math Machine, p.20	●	●				
Same But Different, p.21	●	●				
Cracking the Code, p.22	●					
Calculator Capers, p.24	●					
Tossing Two Dice, p.25	●					
Growing Squares, p.27	●	●				
Clothesline Patterns, p.29	●	●			●	
Indian Headbands, p.31	●	●		●	●	●
Fabric Designers, p.34	●	●				
Veggie Print Patterns, p.37	●	●	●			
Stringing Beads, p.38	●	●			●	●
Paper-Weaving Patterns, p.39	●	●		●		●
Quilt Patterns, p.41	●	●				●
Name Patterns, p.43	●	●			●	
Exploring We Will Go, p.44	●	●		●	●	
Circular Patterns, p.46	●	●		●	●	
Animal Spots, p.47	●	●	●			●
The Four Seasons, p.50	●	●	●			
Beautiful Butterfly Wings, p.52	●	●	●			
Snowflake Symmetry, p.55	●	●	●			
Animal Sleeping Patterns, p.58	●	●	●			
Hand Band, p.60	●			●		
Water Music, p.61	●		●	●		
Pattern Party, p.63	●	●			●	

What Is a Pattern?

You and your children are about to embark on an exciting study of patterns. In this introductory activity, your students will define patterns and have fun displaying their definitions in a pattern around the room.

Most children can describe a pattern better (or at least with less fuss and bother) than most adults can. However, many children think of a pattern only in terms of a line of repeating elements. Patterns can be linear, of course. But they can also cover a two-dimensional space like a wall or a hundreds chart. They can be circular (think of the four seasons), and they can grow or shrink (picture the circles that ripple around a stone dropped in water). They can be symmetrical—or not. Patterns can even consist of movements or sounds, such as musical notes. Mathematicians and scientists often look for patterns in data in order to solve problems. With all this variety, what can be said about patterns in general? They repeat. They have a rule that can be used to describe them. And they are predictable!

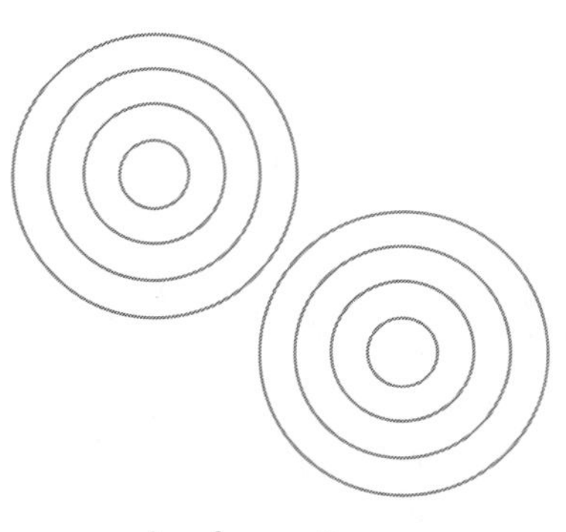

circular pattern

linear pattern

growing pattern

Materials:

- chart paper
- markers
- colored paper (two different colors)

Objectives:

- to discuss what children know about patterns
- to define patterns
- to brainstorm places where patterns are found

Activity

1. Ask if children know what a pattern is. List their responses on chart paper.
2. Have children brainstorm a list of places where patterns are found in their environment. Record their responses and be prepared to add to the list as children's awareness increases. Some possibilities are:

overall patterns
wallpaper
tiles
gift wrap
coats of animals
rugs

clothing patterns
pajamas
socks
skirts
sneaker bottoms
ties

patterns in science
butterfly wings
animal spots
seasons
phases of the moon

overall number patterns
calendar
hundreds chart

blinking patterns
changing street lights
blinking holiday lights
blinking neon signs

weaving patterns
braids
woven mats
friendship bracelets

language/sound patterns
rhyming words in a poem
predictable picture books
bird songs

3. Give each child a piece of paper. Make sure half the class gets paper of one color and half gets paper of the other color.
4. On the colored paper, have each child write a definition of a pattern, starting with the words "A pattern is..." *(Younger children can dictate.)*
5. Invite children to make a pattern around the border of the paper or to illustrate their definitions.
6. Give children a chance to share their definitions with the whole class.
7. Display the results. Hang the papers in a pattern by alternating the colored pages.
8. As you do more pattern work in the activities that follow, refer back to the definitions and add to them.

Patterns to See and Hear

Farm animals provide a perfect blend of simple sight and sound patterns. Use this activity to get children excited about patterns.

Objective:

- to go beyond the linear pattern of ABAB

Materials:

- 2 copies of *Animal Cards* blackline reproducible
- pocket chart *(optional)*
- blank 3" × 3" cards *(optional)*
- markers *(optional)*

Activity

1. Start with at least 12 animal cards *(4 cows, 4 pigs, 4 horses)*. You can use two machine copies of the *Animal Cards* reproducible, or you can have children draw some animal cards. If students create their own cards, make sure all the cows are drawn with black marker, the pigs with pink or red, and the horses with brown. That ensures that the animals can always be identified by color.
2. Let children suggest a pattern for the cards *(for example: pig, horse, cow, pig, horse, cow)*. Arrange the cards in this pattern on the pocket chart. If you don't have a pocket chart, you can tape the cards to a large sheet of posterboard.
3. Review the sound associated with each animal. In unison, recite the sounds according to your pattern: "Oink, neigh, moo, oink, neigh, moo."
4. Use the cards to help children expand their concepts of patterns. Suggest that they go beyond the basic ABAB and ABC/ABC. For example, suggest doubling one or more animals: AAB/AAB or AABB/AABB. Other possibilities are AAABBB/AAABBB, ABCB/ABCB, etc.
5. Discuss what the class has learned about patterns. *(Possible answers include: Patterns can be made of sounds or pictures; we can make many different patterns; patterns are fun.)*

going further:

Make cards for the sounds *and* the animals. Display both, with one set of cards under the other. Or have children create additional animal cards to work with (sheep, dogs, chickens, etc.).

Animal Cards

Cut apart the cards. Use them on the pocket chart to create patterns.

Shrinking Shapes

Children work with squares and triangles to create shrinking patterns.

Objectives:

- to create shrinking patterns with geometric shapes
- to see how shapes relate to each other

Materials:

- *Squares* and *Triangles* blackline reproducibles
- multi-colored paper appropriate for photocopying
- glue and scissors

Preparation:

- Photocopy the squares and triangles onto colored paper. Cut them out for younger children, or invite older children to do their own cutting.

Activity

1. Set out boxes containing squares of different colors and sizes.
2. Invite children to take one square of each size. They can select whatever colors they like, but the activity works best when the four squares are all different colors, or when the squares alternate between two colors *(red/blue/red/blue, for example).*
3. Ask children what they notice about the size and shape of the pieces. *(They are all squares, but they get smaller and smaller.)* Explain that this is called a shrinking pattern. Ask what shape would come next *(either a smaller or larger square).*
4. Invite children to arrange the squares in a pattern on top of each other. Some possibilities are shown below.

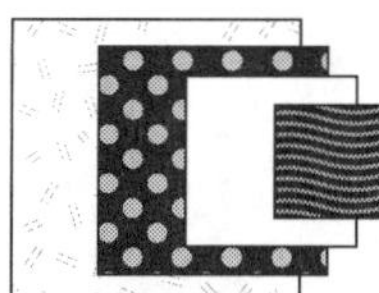
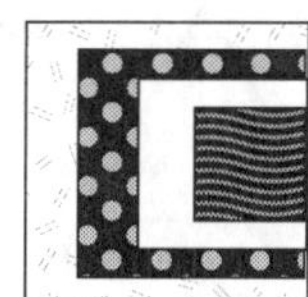

5. Have children glue down their favorite arrangements.
6. To extend the activity, set out boxes containing triangles of different colors and sizes. Have children find different ways of arranging them on top of each other in a pattern. Some possibilities are shown below:

7. Have children glue down their favorites.
8. Discuss what students enjoyed about and learned from this activity. *(Possible responses: Patterns can be made of geometric shapes. Patterns can shrink.)*

Triangles

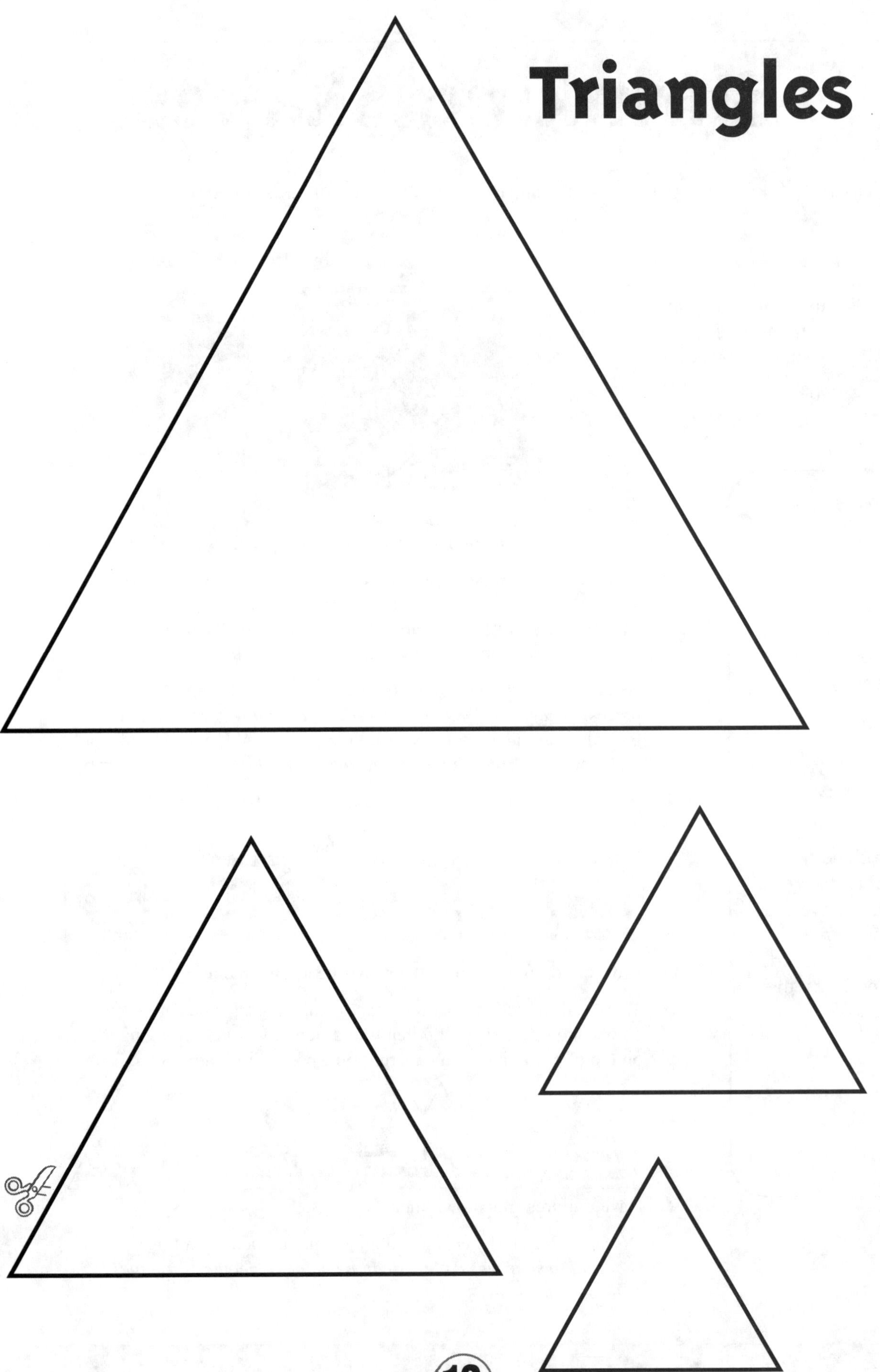

Squares

Calendar Patterns

With its repeating days of the week and its consecutive number pattern, a calendar provides a template for investigating patterns of all kinds. Skip-counting days on a calendar is a wonderful way to begin your investigation!

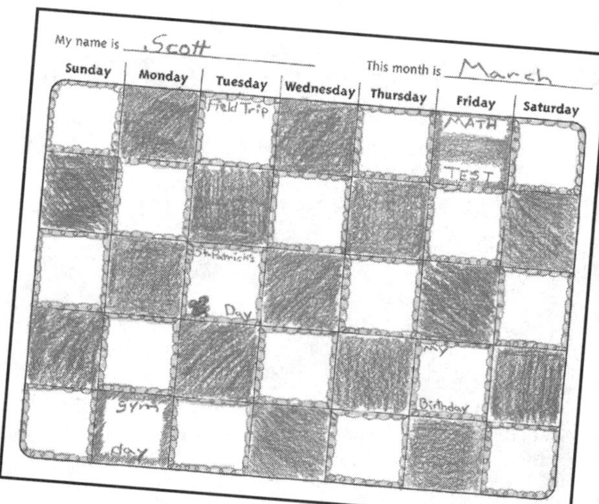

Objectives:

- to skip-count on the calendar
- to make predictions about skip-counting

Materials:

- *Calendar* blackline *(page 15)*
- markers
- crayons
- stickers *(optional)*

Preparation:

- Fill in the *Calendar* blackline with the appropriate numbers for the current month, then make copies for the class.

Activity

1. Pass out a calendar blackline for this month to each child and talk about how it is set up. Where are the days of the week? Where are all the Mondays? Tuesdays? What number does this month start with? How high do the numbers go?
2. Have children use markers to draw pictures on the dates of special events that month—birthdays, holidays, field trips, etc.
3. Introduce a skip-counting pattern for the month. Start with skip-counting by 2s. Have children use crayons to color in the boxes, starting on the 2nd of the month and skip-counting by twos.
4. As children get started, ask them to predict if they will land on the dates of the special events. Take each date and make a prediction. Ask, "If we skip-count by twos, will we land on Juan's birthday?"
5. As children get closer to an event, have them predict again whether they will "land" on it.
6. When everyone has completed the calendar, look it over together. As a group, analyze which special events the children landed on when they skip-counted. Also look at the pattern that was created when they colored in the boxes while they were skip-counting. *(Is it a checkerboard pattern? a diagonal pattern? a striped pattern?)*
7. Ask what students have learned about patterns by looking at the calendar. *(Possible responses: Patterns are predictable. We use patterns when we read a calendar.)*

going further:

Repeat this activity each month, using a different skip-counting pattern each time. Try 3s, 4s, 5s, and so on.

My name is ______________________ This month is ______________________

Sunday	Monday	Tuesday	Wednesday	Thursday	Friday	Saturday

Even-Odd Architects

Use manipulatives to uncover a simple pattern among odd and even numbers.

Objective:

- to discover and describe a pattern involving even and odd numbers

Materials:

- *Even-Odd Architects* blackline reproducible
- Lego™ cubes or other linking cubes

Activity

1. Review the odd and even numbers by reciting them. If students need help remembering, refer to a calendar or hundreds chart.
2. Explain that for this activity the children will be architects. They will work in pairs or groups to construct buildings out of linking cubes.
3. Pass out the *Even-Odd Architects* blackline and linking cubes. Give each pair or group at least 50 linking cubes.
4. Look at the blackline together. Explain that the children will use one cube to build the first building, two cubes for the second and so on. Each building must fit on the two squares pictured on the page, so after the first two cubes are in place, students must build up *(like a tall building)*.
5. Explain that some buildings will have flat roofs and others will have chimneys.
6. Instruct students to build a building with one cube and a building with two cubes.
7. Guide students as they build a building of three cubes and a building of four cubes. The building with four cubes will have a flat roof. The building with three cubes will have a chimney.
8. Have the children complete the rest of the buildings *(numbers 5 through 10 on the reproducible)*. As you observe their work, challenge children to predict what the roofs will look like on the buildings that haven't been built yet.
9. When the groups have finished, work together to find a pattern. Children should notice that buildings made from an even number of cubes have flat roofs, while those made from an odd number of cubes have chimneys.
10. Have students recall their definitions of patterns. What new information can they add now? *(Possible answer: Patterns can be found in odd and even numbers.)*

My name is ______________________________

Even-Odd Architects

1 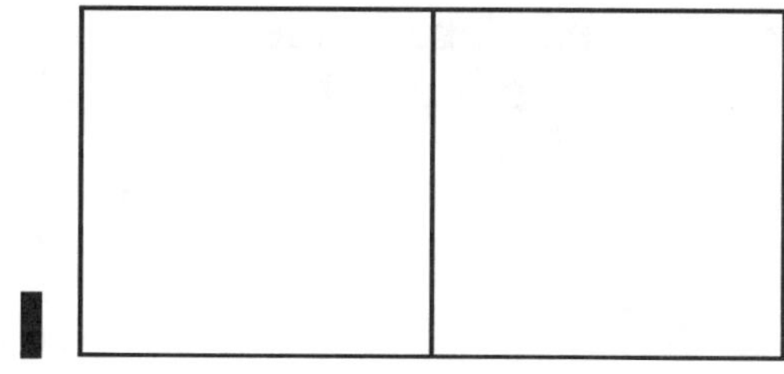

2 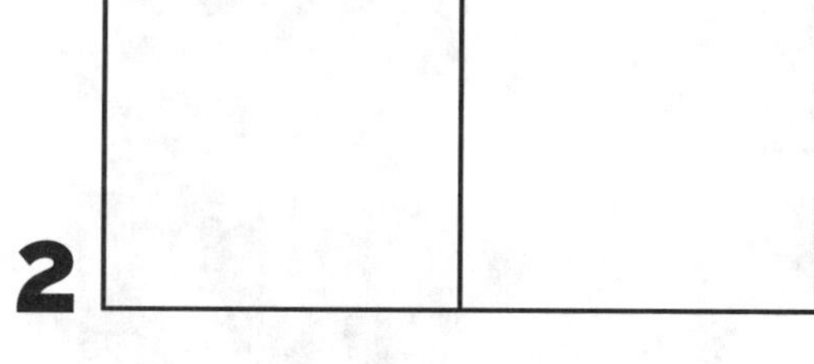

3 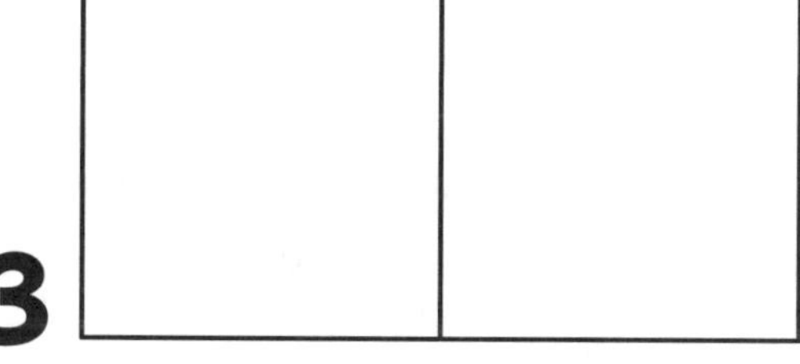

4

5 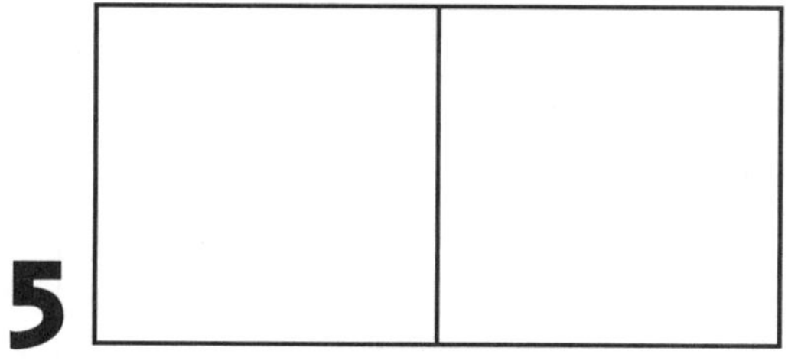

6

7 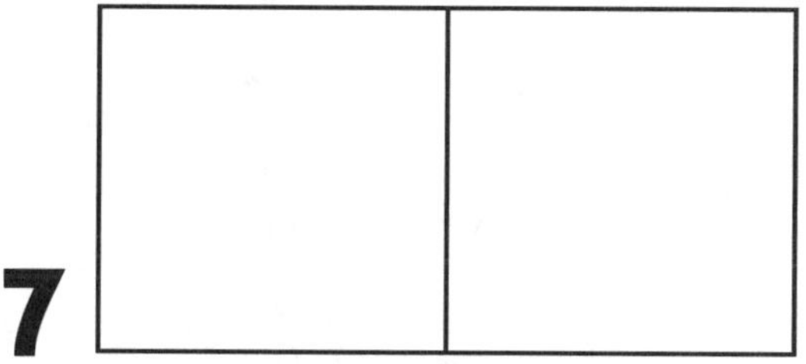

8 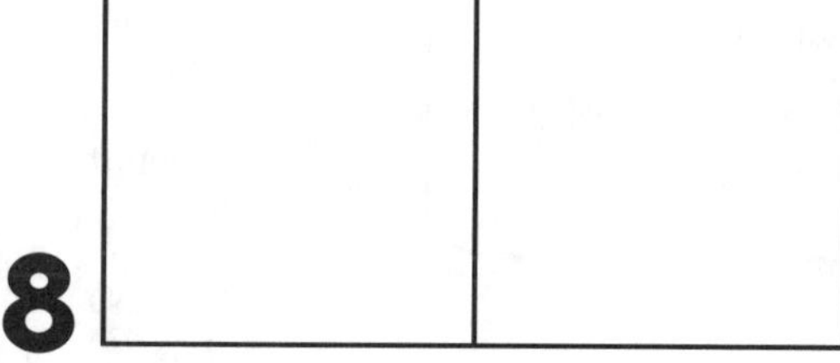

9 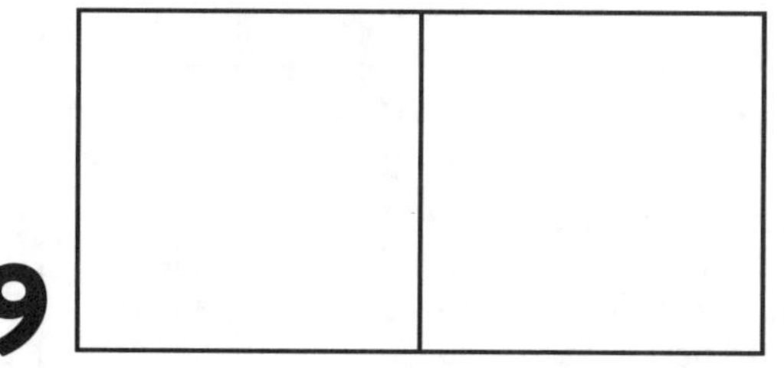

10

Even Plus **Even**

Mathematicians look for patterns in the way numbers work together. Here, student mathematicians decide if there is a pattern when they add even and odd numbers in different combinations.

Objectives:

- to decide if a number pattern exists
- to describe a number pattern

Materials:

- pocket chart and cards saying "Even + Even," "Odd + Odd," "Even + Odd," and "Odd + Even"
- blank pocket chart cards about 3" x 6"
- markers
- linking cubes of 2 colors (optional)

Activity

1. Review odd and even numbers. Explain that children will look for a pattern when they add an even number to an even number, odd to odd, even to odd, and odd to even.
2. Place the four pocket chart labels *(Even + Even, Odd + Odd, Even + Odd, Odd + Even)* in the top pocket of your pocket chart.
3. Invite children to write addition sentences on the blank cards.
4. Have children take turns placing the cards where they belong on the pocket chart. For example, 2 + 3 = 5 goes under the title "Even + Odd."
5. Try to fill up the whole pocket chart. Tell children what is missing. *(Example: We need another "Odd + Odd.")*
6. Let children take turns filling in the pocket chart. Note that numbers ending in zero may be a little confusing for some children since they think of the even numbers starting at 2, rather than 0.
7. When the pocket chart is full, reflect on the pattern that has emerged. Children will find that E + E = E, O + O = E, E+ O = O, O + E = O.
8. Discuss any new ideas about patterns this activity has introduced. *(Possible answer: You make patterns when you add numbers together.)*

going further:

Have children use models made of linking cubes to explain the conclusions.

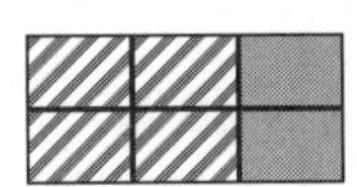

4+2=6

E + E = E because even numbers make rectangles. When you put two together, they form a larger rectangle.

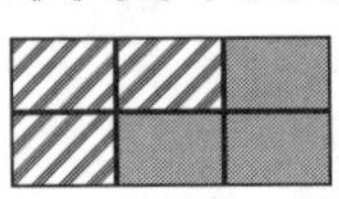

3+3=6

O + O = E because odd numbers produce a rectangle with a loner cube sticking out. The two loner cubes can be placed next to each other, and the result is a rectangle (an even number).

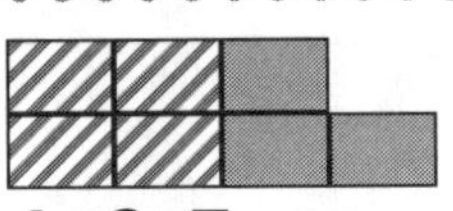

4+3=7

E + O = O When you combine a rectangle and a rectangle with a loner cube sticking out, the result does not make a rectangle.

Tiles to **Hamster Cages**

What do tile floors, honeycombs, and hamster cages have in common? They are examples of tessellations, or patterns made of repeating shapes extending in all directions. These patterns can be found all around, both inside and outside. Let the search begin!

Objectives:

- to find tessellations indoors and outdoors

Materials:

- Pattern Blocks *(Available at teacher supply stores)*
- chart paper for an ongoing list of tessellations

Here are some possibilities for things that tessellate:

Squares
- bathtub tiles
- windows with panes
- wire on animal cages
- brownies cut in a pan

Rectangles
- bathtub tiles
- wooden floor boards
- bricks on a wall or fireplace
- roof tiles
- stamps on a sheet
- baseball cards or photos in an album

Diamonds
- wire fences
- basketball nets

Hexagons
- honeycombs
- chicken wire

Squares and Triangles
- quilt patterns
- rug patterns

Activity

1. Talk about tessellations and the rules they follow: A tessellation consists of one or more shapes that are repeated in a pattern in every direction, without gaps or overlaps. A tessellation can be as complicated as an M. C. Escher drawing or as simple as a tile floor.

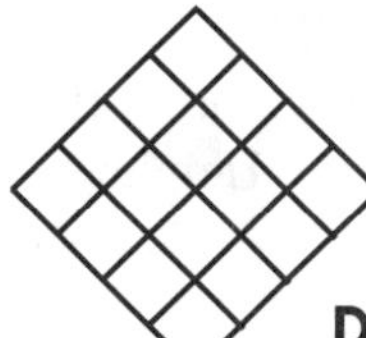

Diamonds and Triangles Tessellate

2. Pass out the Pattern Blocks and let children create a tessellation by repeating one shape in many directions.
3. Look around the classroom to find and record examples of tessellations, such as the ceiling and floor tiles.
4. Go on a tessellation hunt and find all the tessellations you can outdoors. Come back inside and make a list of all the tessellations you found.
5. Have children make lists at home as well.
6. Have each child illustrate one tessellation found in the environment. They can show the tessellation as part of a bigger picture. For example, they might draw a picture of Humpty Dumpty sitting on a brick wall or of a rabbit in a cage made from chicken wire.
7. Ask children to share what they have learned about patterns. *(Possible answer: A tessellation is a special kind of pattern that has a shape repeating itself in all directions.)*

Marvelous **Math** Machine

When children build a Marvelous Math Machine, they will learn to identify number patterns.

Objectives:

- to identify number patterns, also called functions
- to identify the rule that is being used to change one number to another

Materials:

- butcher paper that stretches from a class clothesline to the floor
- blank cards
- markers
- scissors

Preparation:

- Take the piece of butcher paper that represents the Marvelous Math Machine and cut two holes, one for the "in" slot and one for the "out" slot. Label these slots on both sides of the paper.

Activity

1. Hold up the butcher paper and introduce the idea of the Marvelous Math Machine to the children. Explain that when a number is put in, the machine works on the number (by adding to it or subtracting from it) and sends a different number out.
2. Have children come up in groups to decorate the machine. Hang the machine from a clothesline in the classroom.
3. Demonstrate how the machine works by sending a group behind the machine with blank cards. Help them decide on a rule, such as "add two" or "subtract two." Keep this rule a secret from the rest of the class!
4. Invite groups of children in the class to write a number on a blank card and insert it in the "in" slot. *(You might want to put limits on the numbers, such as "less than 50.")*
5. Have the group operating the machine apply their math rule and send a number out the "out" slot.
6. Have one child record all the results using a table with an in and out column. For example, if the rule is "add two," the following will take place.

In	Out
3	5
7	9
10	12
45	47

7. After about 6 numbers have gone in and out of the machine, ask children what the machine is doing. *[Note: "Adding two" is not the only valid answer. For example, children might say the machine is adding 5 and subtracting 3.]*
8. Let other groups operate the machine.
9. Ask children what this machine has to do with patterns. Possible responses are:
   - You can predict what will come out, and that is a pattern.
   - Each in/out table shows a number pattern.
   - The same operation is repeated, making it a pattern.

Same But Different

Having children create the same pattern using different materials can help you assess the depth of children's understanding of patterns.

Objectives:

- to create the same linear pattern using different materials
- to find linear patterns that are similar

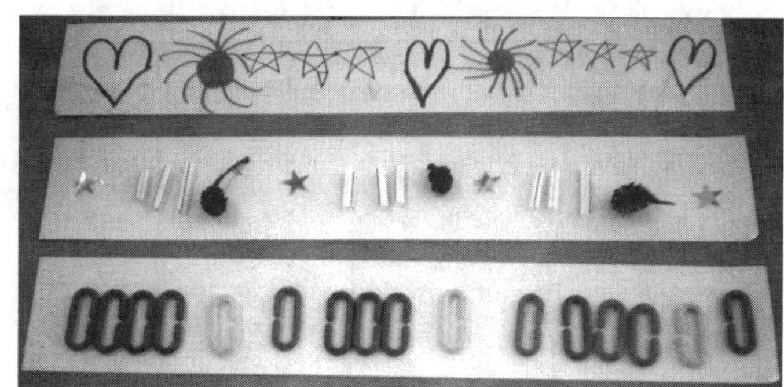

Materials:

- pocket chart; strips of paper 3" x 10" *(Pocket chart strips work well.)*
- math manipulatives such as Color Tiles, Pattern Blocks, Teddy Bear Counters, color links, People Pieces
- objects from nature such as small pine cones, leaves, small acorns
- decorative material such as dots, stars, toothpicks, cut-up straws, and shapes cut from wrapping paper, construction paper, and fabric
- markers, scissors, and glue

Activity

1. Explain that children will be choosing a pattern they like and creating that pattern using different kinds of exciting materials.
2. Divide students into pairs or small groups, and pass out three paper strips to each group. Students will arrange their patterns on these strips.
3. For the first pattern, make color tiles, blocks, or other math manipulatives available to students. Have children arrange the manipulatives in a pattern on one of the paper strips. Note that these manipulatives will not be glued down, so children can rework their pattern as often as they'd like.
4. Once children have created a pattern they like, invite them to use objects from nature or decorative materials *(i.e.., dots and stars)* to recreate the pattern on another strip. These objects can be glued down.
5. Finally, have children draw or write their pattern on the third strip *(they can draw the stars, dots, etc., or write out the words "dot," "star," etc.).*
6. Meet as a class to determine if any of groups came up with the same pattern. One fun way to do this is to display one group's strip *(the one they drew)* and let other groups decide if their pattern is a match for the one displayed. Then proceed to another strip.
7. Discuss what students have learned about patterns. *(Possible answer: The same pattern can be made of many different materials.)*

note: It can be difficult for students to compare their patterns with other children's patterns. Children can use claps and snaps, sounds, or letters (ABBABB) to verify that two patterns are indeed the same. You may want to walk around the room as students work, helping each group as needed.

Cracking the Code

One of the most common pattern activities—extending a pattern—is often presented in a misleading way. Children often get the idea that there is only one way to complete the pattern. This is most likely not true.

Objectives:

- to extend number patterns
- to show that patterns can be extended in different ways

1, 3, 5, 7, __, __, __, __, could be
1, 3, 5, 7, 11, 13, 15, ...
1, 3, 5, 7, 1, 3, 5, 7, ...
1, 3, 5, 7, 7, 5, 3, 1, ...
1, 3, 5, 7, 1, 1, 3, 3, 5, 5, 7, 7, ...
There are so many possibilities!

Materials:

- ▲ *Crack the Code* blackline reproducible

Activity

1. Explain that this activity is about cracking a code by finding a pattern.
2. Show the class some number patterns and work on "cracking the code" together:

   5, 6, 7, _____, _____ , _____

   4, 6, 8, 10, _____, _____ , _____

   Be sure students know that there are many ways that the patterns could be extended.
3. Pass out the *Crack the Code* blackline and look it over together.
4. Have children fill in the blanks individually or in pairs.
5. When everyone is ready, discuss the possible answers as a class. Show your enthusiasm if children come up with a variety of answers.
6. Save time at the end for children to share the number patterns they made up. Children can present the first four numbers of their patterns and the class can guess the rest.
7. Discuss the definition of "pattern." What new things can students say about patterns after this activity? *(Possible answer: Patterns can be tricky—there can be many right ways to continue a pattern.)*

going further:

Let children make up more number patterns for a partner to complete.

My name is ______________________________

Crack the Code

There is more than one way to finish each pattern. Find one way.

2, 4, 6, 8, _____, _____, _____, _____, _____, _____

1, 3, 5, 7, _____, _____, _____, _____, _____, _____

1, 1, 2, 2, 3, 3, _____, _____, _____, _____, _____, _____

7, 8, 9, 7, 8, 9 _____, _____, _____, _____, _____, _____

10, 9, 8, 7, _____, _____, _____, _____, _____, _____

5, 10, 15, 20, _____, _____, _____, _____, _____, _____

10, 20, 30, 40, _____, _____, _____, _____, _____, _____

14, 16, 18, 20, _____, _____, _____, _____, _____, _____

1, 2, 1, 2, 3, 1, 2, 3, 4, _____, _____, _____, _____, _____

Make up your own number pattern:

____, ____, ____, ____, ____, ____, ____, ____, ____

Calculator Capers

Most calculators have a "constant" function that allows a child to skip count with ease. When children recognize the pattern, they can anticipate the number that will appear next.

Objectives:

- to play with skip-counting patterns on the calculator

Materials:

▲ calculator

Activity

1. Teach children how to use the constant function on the calculator. Start with counting by twos. Have children key in [+][2][=] to get 2. If they press [=] again, they will get 4. As a class, anticipate the next number and then press [=]. Keep on going. *(These are the even numbers!)*
2. Now it's time to count by threes. Clear the calculator, then key in [+][3][=] together. Have children anticipate the next number before pressing [=] each time.
3. Try counting by 10s. Count by 10s to 100.
4. Then try some larger numbers. Count by 12s to 108 and beyond. Count by 15s and 20s. Take suggestions from the children.
5. For older students, present a real context: Suppose you sleep 11 hours in one night. How many hours do you sleep in 2 nights, 3 nights, 4 nights, 5 nights *(22, 33, 44, 55)*. Children can use the constant function to find the answer. They will be able to anticipate the answers before they press the [=] key again.

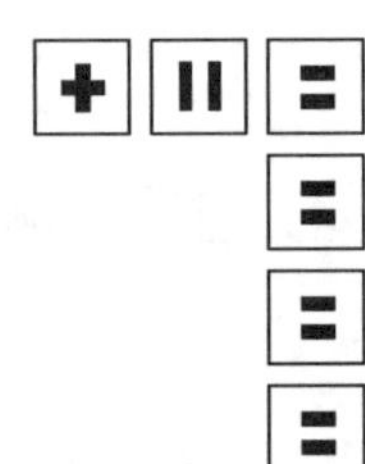

6. As a class, talk about what the calculator is doing in all these cases. *(The calculator has been programmed to skip-count!)*
7. Ask what the calculator has taught students about patterns. *(Possible answer: Skip counting is an example of a pattern.)*

going further:

Use calculator skip counting to solve other real-life questions. For example, there are 24 hours in one day. How many hours in 2 days, 3 days, 4 days, 5 days?

Tossing Two Dice

Many games involve tossing two dice. Tell students that they can predict which numbers they are most likely to roll. How? By finding patterns!

Objective:

- to use discrete math to find all possible outcomes

Materials:

- *Tossing Dice* black-line reproducible
- two dice for each pair of children *(If possible, give each pair two dice of different colors or sizes.)*

Activity

1. Have children name all the numbers that can be tossed on one die *(1 through 6)*. Explain that now students will find all the possible ways that two dice can land when tossed.
2. Pass out and discuss the *Tossing Dice* blackline. First, find the only way to toss a 2 *(1 + 1)* and have everyone record it. Ask why a 1 can't be tossed with two dice.
3. Go on to the number 3 on the blackline. Using two dice of different sizes or colors, show why rolling 1 and 2 is different from rolling 2 and 1. *(Each die has its own 1 and its own 2.)* Have students record 2 + 1 and 1 + 2 on the blackline as different ways to roll a 3.

   example:

2	1+1	
3	2+1	1+2

4. Tell children to try numbers 4 through 12 on the blackline. They should look for all the ways they can roll each number.
5. After children have been working for a few minutes, review the idea that only numbers 1 through 6 can be rolled on a die. *(Undoubtedly, some students will have written 7+ 1 for 8.)*
6. Have children show you any patterns that are emerging. A triangle shape should begin to form.

   example:

4	1+3	2+2	3+1	
5	1+4	2+3	3+2	4+1

7. Have children describe the pattern they see. *(The lowest and highest numbers have the fewest roll combinations. There are many ways to roll the middle numbers, such as 6, 7, and 8.)*
8. Ask students to explain what they have learned about patterns by filling in the dice chart. *(Possible answer: Patterns can be found even in games.)*

Tossing Dice

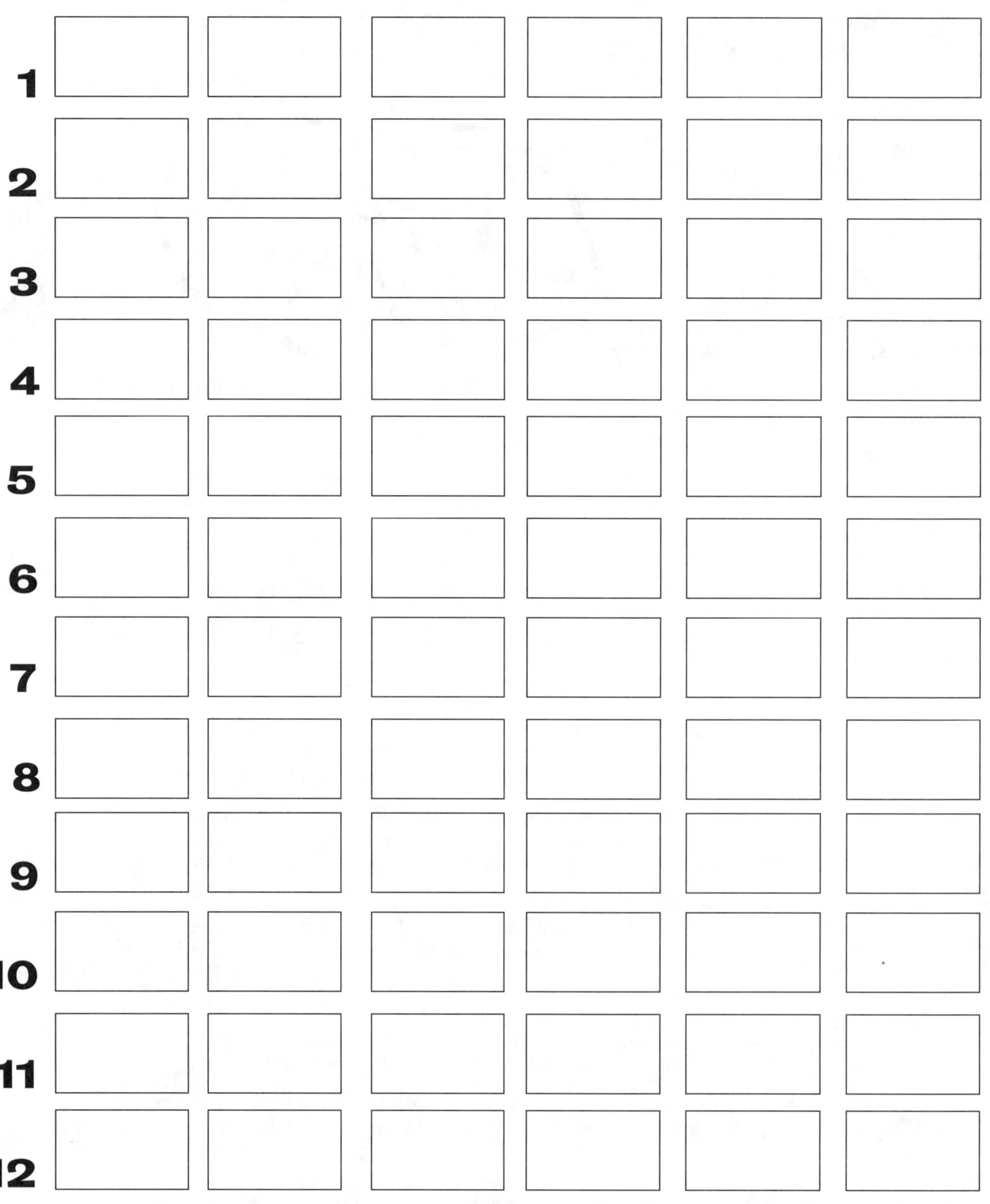

Growing Squares

The square numbers (4, 9, 16, ...) are an example of a growing pattern. Making models of squares is a concrete way for students to explore this type of pattern.

Objectives:

- to create a growing pattern

Materials:

- color tiles or linking cubes
- blank paper

Activity

1. Explain that children will make patterns that grow. Have children describe what that means. *(Example: Patterns that get bigger.)*
2. Pass out the color tiles to pairs of children. Each pair will need at least 14 tiles.
3. Show one tile and explain that one tile by itself is a small square. Point out that it is the same length on each side.
4. Put two tiles together and ask, "Is this a square?" *(no)*. Put three tiles together and ask again *(no)*. Put four tiles together and ask again if this is a square *(yes)*.
5. Have children use color tiles to build these two squares *(one tile and four tiles)* on blank paper.
6. Ask children to build a square using 9 tiles. Keep the first two squares kept intact so that children can see the pattern of growth.

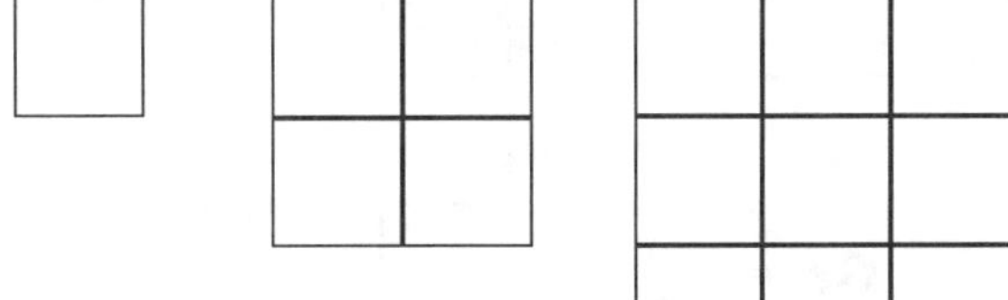

Growing Squares

7. To begin finding patterns, ask children to look at each square and count the number of color tiles in each row.

8. Together, describe the pattern. *(The squares grow bigger and bigger when we add tiles to the rows. There must be the same number of tiles in each row for the shape to be a square.)*

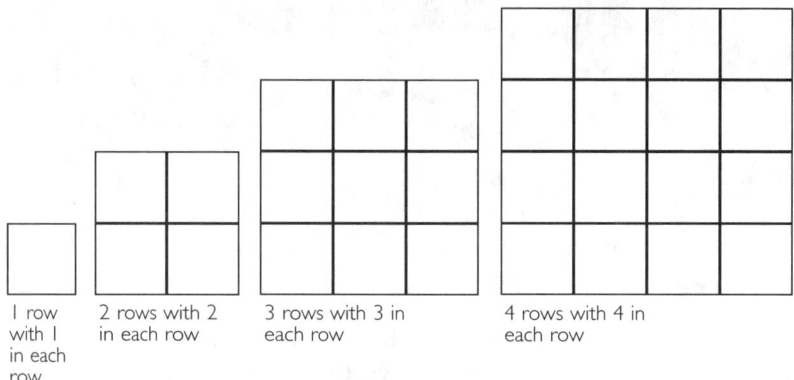

9. Ask children about the next square that hasn't been built yet. Let them predict how many tiles would be in each row *(four)*.

10. Ask what children have learned about patterns with this activity. *(Possible answer: Patterns can grow, or get bigger.)*

going further:

Suggest that students construct "growing staircases" with the tiles or "growing circles" with buttons or other round manipulatives.

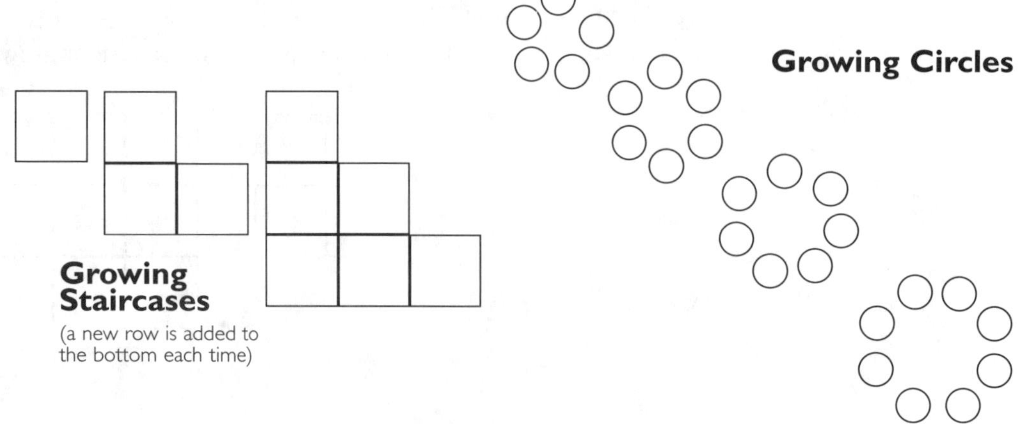

Clothesline Patterns

Everyday life is full of fun patterns. Socks hung to dry on a clothesline are one bright example.

Objectives:

- to recognize and describe visual patterns
- to create a linear visual pattern

Materials:

- *Socks* blackline reproducible
- 5 1/2" x 17" paper for drawing clothesline *(one sheet for each pair of students)*
- glue
- scissors
- old socks collected from home
- string and clothespins

Activity

1. Have children bring old socks from home that no longer have mates. Encourage children to describe the patterns on the socks and to sort the socks in different ways *(color, size, stripes/no stripes, etc.)*.
2. Have the children create a clothesline pattern. Hang the socks up on a string with clothespins, or place the string and socks on the floor.
3. Next students will create their own clotheslines. Pair up the children and distribute the *Socks* blackline and the "clothesline" paper. Have children position the paper horizontally and draw a clothesline across it.
4. Invite students to cut out the socks from the blackline. Have each partner decorate four socks, using the same pattern for all four.
5. Give children time to use their socks to make patterns on the clothesline. Tell them that they don't have to use all the socks. If they need more socks to complete the pattern, they can use another *Socks* blackline. *(Note: Students may be inclined to go with the familiar pattern ABAB. Point out that students can use their imaginations: BBABBABBA, etc. They can also point the toes right and left in a pattern.)*
6. Ask children to glue down their final patterns.
7. Have children display their completed patterns. Ask pairs to circulate around the room and figure out what comes next on each clothesline.
8. Ask students what they have learned about patterns. *(Possible answer: Socks in a row are an example of a linear pattern.)*

literature link:

Sorting All Sorts of Socks by Betsy Franco (Creative Publications, 1997) and the accompanying Attribute Socks will stir up excitement about socks. Or try *A Pair of Socks* by Stuart J. Murphy (Scholastic MathStart, 1996).

Socks

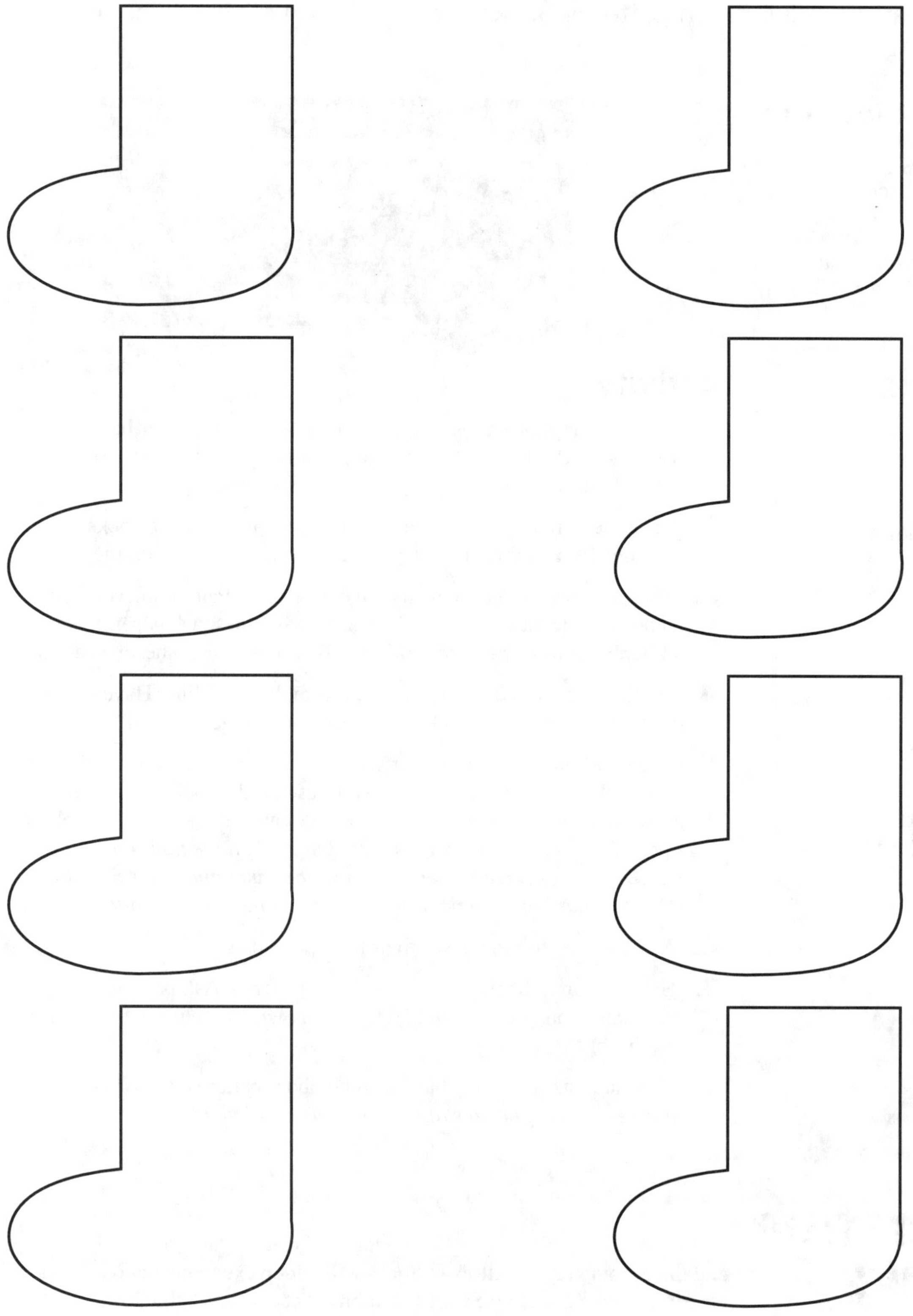

Indian Headbands

When American Indians gather at traditional powwows, some wear beautiful headbands made of tiny beads arranged in linear and circular patterns. This activity features the designs of the Ponca, who are Plains Indians, and of the Apache, who are from the Southwest.

Objectives:

- to create a linear pattern
- to create a circular pattern
- to create a surrounding pattern (optional)

Materials:

- ▲ *American Indian Designs* blackline reproducible
- ▲ strips of tag board for the headbands 1 1/2" x 15" *(pocket chart strips work well, if cut in half lengthwise)*
- ▲ tag board circles approximately 3" across
- ▲ markers, pencils, tape, scissors, glue
- ▲ *Ten Little Rabbits* by Virginia Grossman and Sylvia Long (Chronicle Books, 1991) *(optional)*
- ▲ drums or tin cans *(optional)*

Activity

1. Pass out the headband strips. Let partners help each other measure and cut the headbands to fit their heads. Be sure they overlap the ends of the headband before deciding where to cut.
2. Distribute the *American Indian Designs* blackline. Have children look at the picture of the boy wearing a headband at the top of the page.
3. Explain to students that there is a pattern around the band.
4. Have children look over the patterns on the blackline. Discuss the designs students find most interesting. You may wish to explain to students that some of the patterns are called surrounding patterns. *(See right.)*

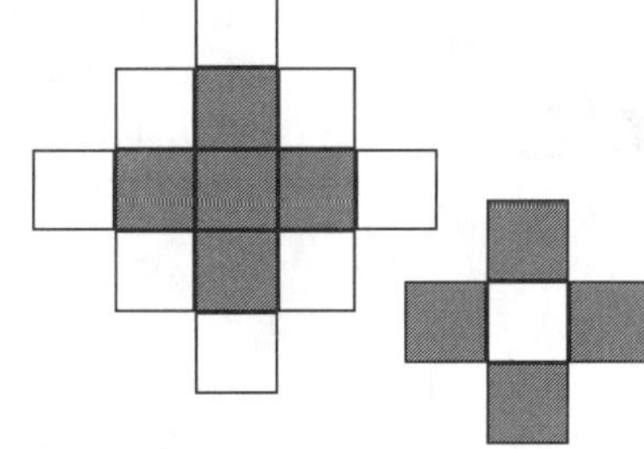

5. Ask children to pick either the Apache or the Ponca and choose 2 or 3 designs they like. They will be drawing these on their headbands in a pattern. *(Students should not use the circle designs at the bottom of the page. These will be used for the circular piece in the front of the headband.)*

Indian Headbands

6. Discuss the many pattern possibilities: AAB/AAB, AABB/AABB, AABC/AABC, etc. Children may want to use Color Tiles to try out their patterns before starting.

7. Children may want to sketch their designs in pencil on the headbands and then go over them with markers. Encourage students to use the bright yet earthy colors common to Native American artwork: red, yellow, brown, black, and some green.

8. Once the bands are complete, children can start on the circular piece that is at the front of the headband. The blackline shows both an Apache and a Ponca circular design. Invite children to copy the circular design from the blackline or to make one up. Children might want to also cut fringe around the edge of the circle, which creates another circular pattern.

9. Glue or tape the circles to the headbands. Help children place their headbands around their heads and tape the ends together.

10. As a culminating activity, have all the children sit in a circle wearing their headbands. Have a brief period of silence and then pass out drums or tin cans for a drumming session.

11. Add some new details to children's original definitions of patterns based on this activity. *(Possibilities include: Patterns are used by different cultures. Patterns are used in clothing. Patterns can go in a line or in a circle.)*

literature link:

Reading the book *Ten Little Rabbits* by Virginia Grossman and Sylvia Long serves as a rich introduction or addition to this activity. Explain that the children will be creating American Indian headbands with designs similar to those in the book.

going further:

In the Amazon rain forest in South America, some native people wear headbands and other headpieces made from feathers. If you are studying the rain forest, you may want to have children make headbands using multicolored paper feathers. The feathers could be arranged in a pattern.

American Indian Designs

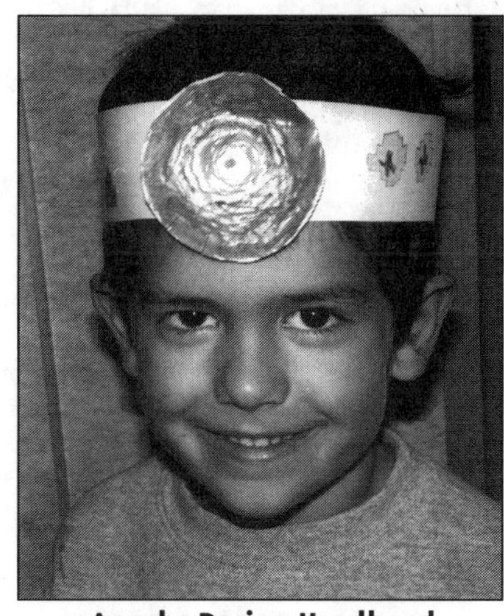
Apache Design Headband

Apache Designs

Ponca Designs

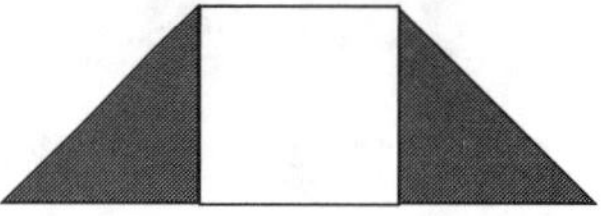

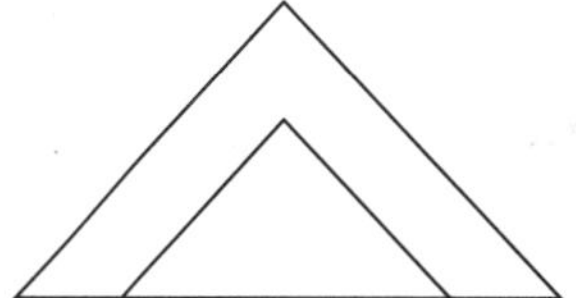

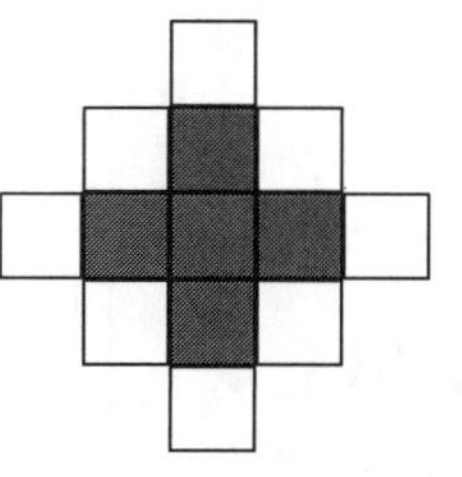

Apache Circle Design

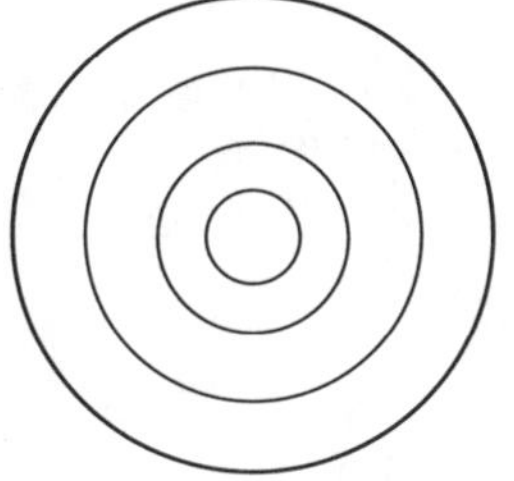

Ponca Circle Design

Teddy Bear Fabric Designs

Many children think of patterns as being only linear. Creating fabric to dress a teddy bear will give children a chance to explore an overall pattern in a fun context.

Objectives:

- to create overall (two-dimensional) patterns
- to use an overall pattern in a practical context

Materials:

- *Teddy Bear* blackline
- *Teddy Bear Clothes* blackline
- markers, scissors, glue
- stamps and stamp pads *(optional)*

Preparation:

- Have samples of fabric, wrapping paper, etc. to show. Making a model of a bear with patterned clothing would also be helpful. For younger students, cut out bears in advance.

Activity

1. Explain that children will be designing fabric for teddy bear clothing using overall patterns.
2. Introduce the word "overall." *(You may need to explain that in this case it does not mean pants with straps over the shoulders.)* Look around the room and point out examples of overall patterns on children's clothing. Say, for example, "Chrissy has polka dots all over her jumper. Dan has stripes all over his shirt. These are examples of overall patterns."
3. If you wish, show other samples of overall patterns using wrapping paper, fabrics, origami paper, or wallpaper samples. Have children brainstorm the characteristics of an overall pattern. *(Some shape or design is repeated over the whole space. The colors are repeated as well.)*
4. Pass out one bear and the *Teddy Bear Clothes* blackline to each child. Make markers, crayons, and scissors available.
5. Have students color their bears brown. *(An alternative is to copy the Teddy Bear blackline onto brown paper.)*
6. Brainstorm "fabric" designs to decorate the bears' clothes — stars, dots, stripes, plaids, flowers, geometric shapes, animals, sports symbols, etc. Children can also use stamps.
7. Accessories—purses, skateboards, etc.—can be made freehand.
8. Help children cut out the clothing and glue it on the bears. They can use a marker to draw in the bear's face.
9. Talk about what students have learned in doing this activity. *(Possible answers: Clothes often have patterns. An overall pattern is a pattern that covers a whole space.)*

Teddy Bear Clothing

Veggie Print Patterns

Fruits and vegetables are not only good for you; they are also beautiful. This activity uses the cross-sections of several easy-to-find fruits and veggies. When pressed on ink pads (or dipped in tempura paint) and stamped, these cross-sections make lovely patterns.

Objectives:

- to create an overall or circular pattern

Materials:

- ▲ celery, apple, cucumber, pepper, onion
- ▲ knife
- ▲ ink pads of different colors or tempura paint in shallow containers
- ▲ large white paper (about 12" x 15" or 11" x 17")

Preparation:

- ▲ Cut up the produce so that cross-sections are revealed. Lay each fruit or vegetable stamp next to an ink pad or a container of tempura paint.

Activity

1. Explain that children will be using veggies and fruits to print in a pattern.
2. Have children guess and sketch what the cross-section of each food looks like before showing it to them.
3. Demonstrate the printing process—dipping the veggie onto the pad or into the paint, pressing down hard on the paper, and returning the veggie to its original position.
4. Ask for ideas about how to print in a pattern. Examples:

```
A B A B
C C C C
A B A B
C C C C
```

```
A B A
B A B
A B A
```

```
A B C A B C
A B C A B C
A B C A B C
```

```
   C C C C
 C  B   B  C
C  B  A  B  C
C   B   B   C
   C C C C
```

```
A A A
B B B
A A A
```

```
A A B B
B B A A
A A B B
```

5. Help students start their own patterns. Auditory learners will find it helpful to verbalize their patterns: "Apple, apple, pepper, apple, apple, pepper."
6. Display the results on a clothesline or wall.

going further:

Children can turn their work into a poster titled, "Eat Your Fruits and Veggies," and bring the poster home as a reminder of good eating habits. Or have students use their printed papers as homemade gift wrap.

Stringing Beads

Beading in patterns started thousands of years ago, and is used in many cultures around the world. Children can carry on this tradition by creating their own beaded necklaces from colored macaroni.

Objective:

- to create a linear pattern or a growing pattern using beads

Materials:

- string *(about 34" long)* with tape twirled around the ends to keep "beads" from sliding off
- small and large macaroni *(elbow noodles and ziti work well)*
- small paperclips, food dye, rubbing alcohol, resealable bags.

Preparation:

- Color the macaroni by shaking it in a plastic bag with rubbing alcohol and food dye.

Activity

1. Sort the small macaroni into containers according to color. Put large macaroni onto small paper clips and place in a container. *(Paper clips allow these "beads" to dangle from the string. If you are short on time, you can have students string the macaroni lengthwise instead.)*

Ziti on a paper clip

2. Pass out string and make the macaroni available so children can begin. Explain that children will be stringing the macaroni in a pattern.
3. If you'd like, show children how to make a necklace with a growing pattern, like the one at the right. Explain that this is a growing pattern because the number of beads of each color gets larger and larger. ABBCCCDDDDEEEEE is repeated on each side of the center bead

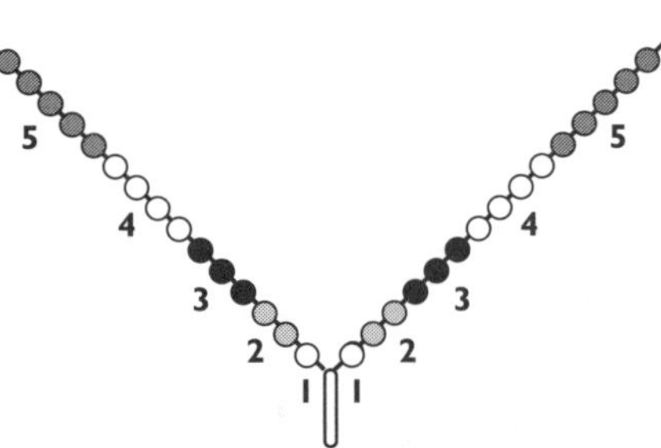

4. When the necklaces are done, tie ends together with a square knot.
5. Have children model their necklaces and describe the patterns they used.
6. Discuss any new ideas about patterns the children have had while creating the necklaces. *(Possible responses: Patterns are in jewelry. Patterns can grow.)*

literature link:

A String of Beads by Margarette S. Reid (Dutton Children's Books, 1997) introduces the history of beads. The author explains that in Africa, people made beads from objects that were readily available. By making necklaces from macaroni, children are in a sense carrying on this African tradition.

Paper-Weaving Patterns

Children may have woven mats before, but not like this! Weaving is a nice example of a pattern because it involves both a visual and a verbal pattern.

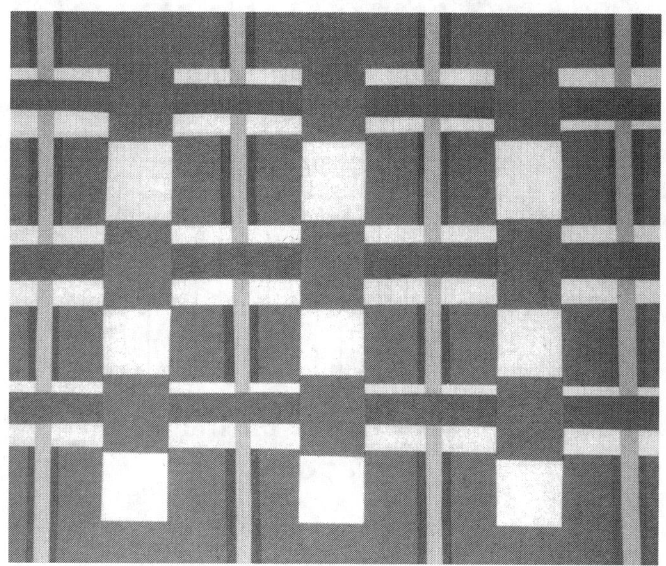

Objectives:

- to create overall patterns by weaving
- to verbalize a pattern

Materials:

- ▲ construction paper for the background *(8 1/2" x 11")*
- ▲ strips of white paper 1"x11"
- ▲ strips of colored construction paper *(11" long with widths less than 1")*
- ▲ scissors and glue

Preparation:

- ▲ For the initial weaving activity, prepare the construction paper by folding it in half, cutting lines about 1" apart, then unfolding it.

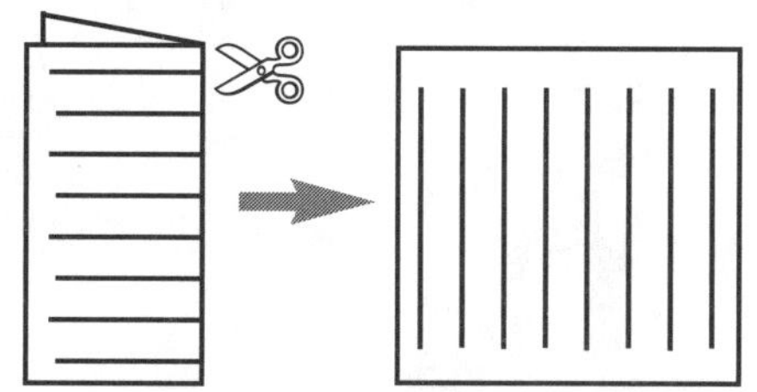

Activity

1. Have children discuss things that can be woven: baskets, clothing, mats, rugs. Tell them that they will be weaving mats.
2. Hand out white strips and pre-cut construction paper.
3. Model and help children weave in an "over, under, over, under..." pattern, moving the white strips over and under the slots in the construction paper. Have the children verbalize the pattern as they weave. Show children how the second row starts with under instead of over: "under, over, under, over..."
4. When mats are complete, have children glue, tape, or staple the ends of the strips that were woven through the mat.
5. Talk about why the mats are examples of patterns. *(Possible answer: Because the strips go "over" and "under" the colored paper in a repeating, predictable way.)*

Paper-Weaving Patterns

going further:

If your students are ready for a challenge, demonstrate some unusual ways of weaving.

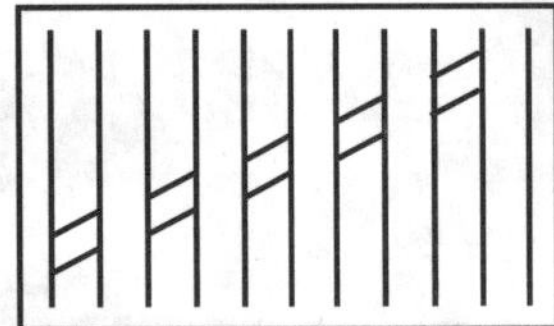

Weave on the diagonal

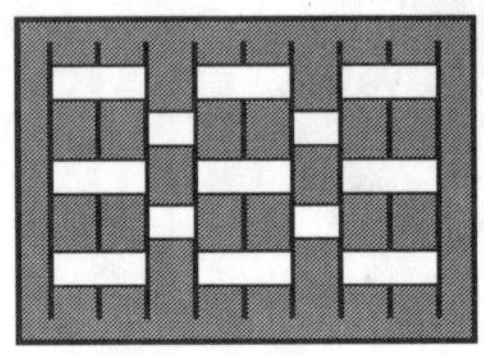

Weave in a different pattern

You will need some longer strips to weave on the diagonal. Start in the middle. Cut off ends of strips that hang off the mat.

Weave a Scottish tartan (plaid)

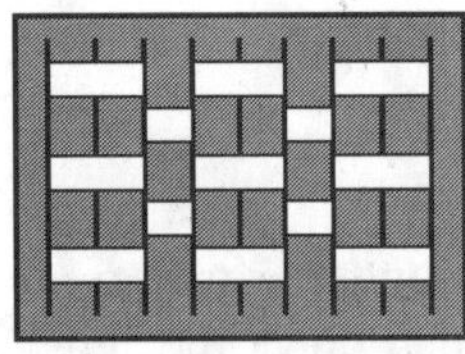

a. Weave across with white strips.

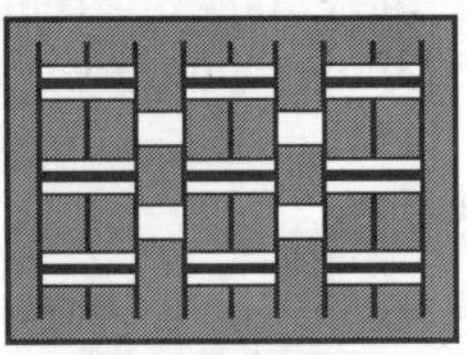

b. Weave across with thinner, colored strips on top of the white strips.

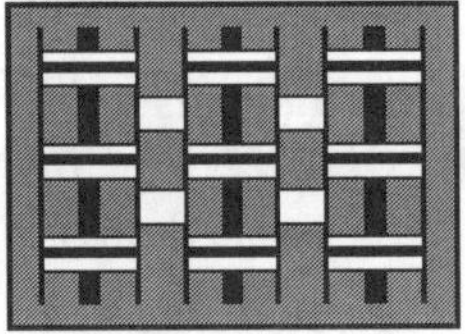

c. Weave down with thinner, dark strips.

Quilt Patterns

A quilter works with patterns in several ways. The designs of the squares themselves, such as the pinwheel design, have repeating elements. Then, when the squares are sewn together to make a quilt, a particular design may be repeated over and over.

Objectives:

- to create a quilt pattern on a grid
- to arrange blocks on a quilt in a checkerboard pattern

Materials:

- *Four-Patch* blackline reproducible
- squares and triangles cut from gift wrap *(2" x 2" squares and triangles made by cutting these squares in half diagonally)*
- squares cut from construction paper (2" x 2", all the same color)

  (Note: You can use the squares and triangles on page 42 as a template.)
- posterboard on which to mount the quilt squares

Preparation:

You may wish to make some four-patches in advance to share with students.

Activity

1. Have children relate what they know about quilts and quilt designs.
2. Introduce the *Four-Patch* template.
3. Show children how the precut triangles and squares can be arranged on the template to form different quilt designs. Show your sample designs, and have the children name the designs.

Pinwheel

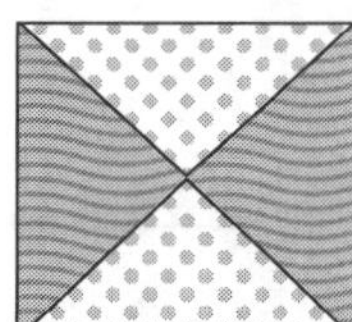

Hourglass

Flock of Birds

4. Pass out a *Four-Patch* template to each child. Invite children to use the squares and triangles made of gift wrap to design quilt blocks.
5. When children have a design they like, they can glue down the pieces and cut out their finished quilt block.
6. Alternate the children's quilt blocks and the plain squares cut from construction paper to make a checkerboard quilt pattern on a piece of posterboard. To accommodate all the children's work, you may need to make two quilts. Let the children help you arrange the squares so that they are pleasing to the eye. For example, you may want to make sure that the colors are dispersed throughout, rather than having all the predominantly yellow blocks all clustered together.
7. Discuss what students have learned about patterns. *(Possible response: A quilt is one kind of pattern. It has patterns inside the squares and a big pattern on the whole quilt.)*

Quilt Template

For children to create a quilt block

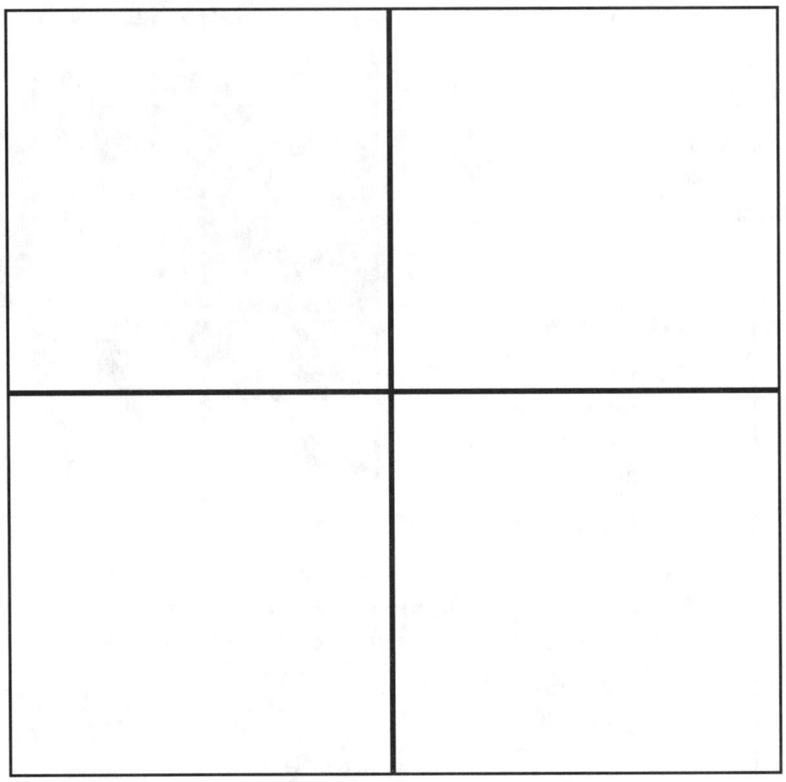

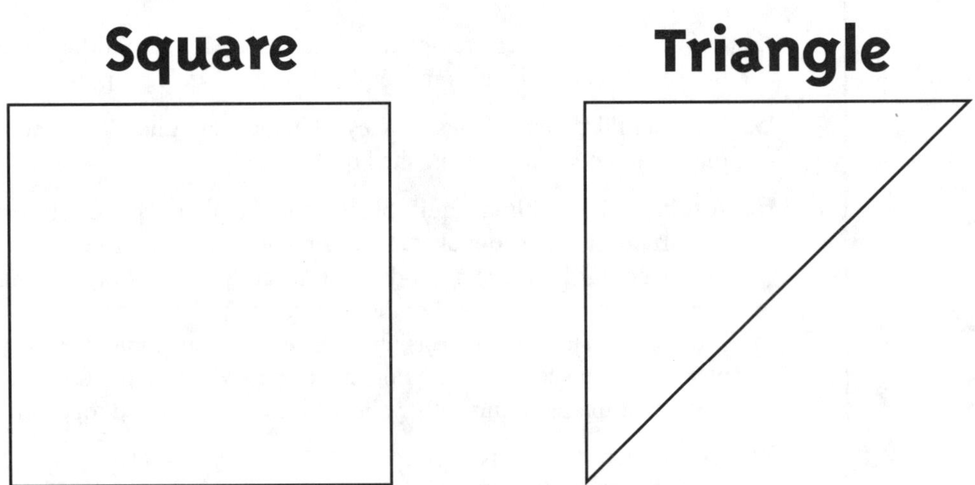

Name Patterns

A child's name is a very personal and familiar word to her or him, making it perfect for spotting patterns.

Objectives:

- to create and recognize a pattern on a matrix
- to identify vowels

Materials:

- inch grid-paper, custom-cut into a rectangle for each child *(The paper should be three spaces deep and one space longer than the child's first name. Be sure to create a rectangle for your own name.)*
- six containers of crayons, each with one color *(Write a different vowel on each container.)*

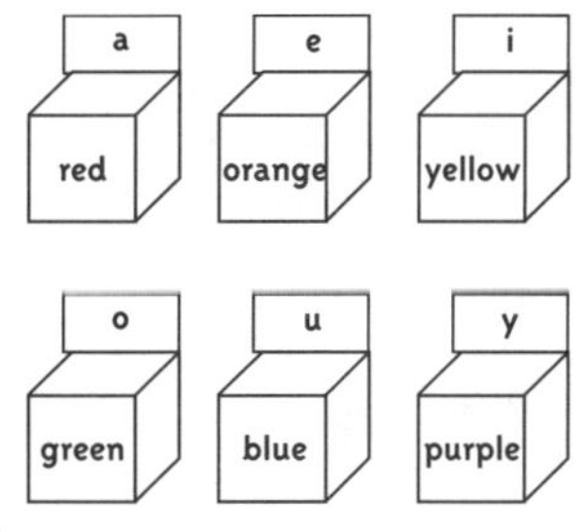

Activity

1. Show the children a grid and explain that they will be writing their names over and over again until the paper is filled up. Explain that they will be doing something strange—leaving no spaces between words.
2. Model the activity using your own name. Write all of the letters in black. Color in all the squares with vowels using the correct color.

J	O	E	J
O	E	J	O
E	J	O	E

3. Use the crayon boxes to review the six vowels *(a, e, i, o, u, sometimes y)* and point out that almost everyone has at least one vowel in their first name. *(If a student goes by initials, such as J. T., ask what the first initial stands for.)*
4. While children are working on their name patterns, circulate and question them about the emerging diagonal pattern.
5. When children are finished, discuss the diagonal patterns together. A few children may have a double vowel, making the diagonal stripe thicker. *(Examples: Lee, Brook, Aaron, Doreen)*
6. Discuss what the class has learned about patterns. *(Possible answers: There are patterns in our names. A matrix or grid makes a pattern stand out.)*

going further:

Create a graph showing the number of letters in students' names. Or, graph the number of vowels in students' names. Look for patterns!

Exploring We Will Go

Language patterns are frequently woven into story books.

Objectives:

- to recognize language patterns in picture books
- to create a poem with a language pattern

Materials:

- *A-Hunting We Will Go* by John Langstaff (A Margaret K. McElderry Book, Atheneum, 1974)
- *Exploring We Will Go* blackline
- watercolors, pen with black ink
- construction paper for a book cover
- pocket chart strips *(optional)*

Preparation:

Make copies of the blackline for the class, and cut each along the line to form a boot shape. Cut the construction paper into the same shape for the cover.

Activity

1. Talk about how patterns are even in story books. Explain that you will be reading *A-Hunting We Will Go* and the children will be hunting for a pattern in the words.
2. Read *A-Hunting We Will Go* aloud. After a few pages, invite children to recite the book along with you. Show the pictures, which de-emphasize the idea of hunting in the literal sense.
3. Let children explain why they were able to read the book along with you without seeing the text. *(The text is written in a pattern!)*
4. Explore the rhyme pattern in the book by saying aloud the last word in each line. The rhyming pattern is: A/A/B/B/A.
5. Explain that everyone will be making a page for a class book entitled *Exploring We Will Go*, and that the students' book will have the same rhyme pattern as the book you just read.
6. Use the pocket chart or chart paper to write out the poetry frame the children will be using. Emphasize the word exploring. Ask what tools children could use for exploring *(binoculars, walking stick, camera).*

   Exploring we will go,
   Exploring we will go,
   We'll find a _______,
   and _____________,
   and then we'll let it go.
7. Brainstorm some animals and rhyming words that children could use in their verses: frog (log dog, jog), ant (plant, aunt), cow (bow, plow, chow), sheep (sleep, jeep, heap) etc.
8. Hand out a pre-cut boot to every child. Have children fill in the blanks to create a poem with the same pattern as the book.
9. Invite children to illustrate their poems with pen and watercolors and share their poems with the class. Then compile the poems into a book for the classroom library.
10. Discuss new ideas about patterns students have taken from this activity. *(Possible answers: Some patterns are in books. There are rhyming patterns.)*

My name is ______________________

Exploring we will go,
Exploring we will go,
We'll find a __________,
and ____________________,
and then we'll let it go.

Circular Patterns In **Picture Books**

Children will understand what a circular pattern is in literature after reading the charming picture book, *If You Give a Mouse a Cookie*, and writing their own version of this tale.

Objectives:

- to recognize a circular pattern in a picture book
- to create a similar circular pattern

Materials:

- *If You Give a Mouse a Cookie* by Laura Joffe Numeroff (HarperCollins, 1985)
- chart paper
- construction paper
- scissors and marker

Activity

1. Draw a circle, and talk about circles. *(A circle goes around and around. If you start somewhere on a circle and walk all the way around the circle, you will come back to the start.)*
2. Tell children that the book *If You Give a Mouse a Cookie* starts and ends in the same way. It goes around in a circle. Read the story aloud. Stress the ending, in which the story starts all over again.
3. Let children begin brainstorming a take-off on the story featuring a different animal, such as a bunny. Help students use the language pattern from the original book: "If you..., then...."
4. On chart paper, write out the children's version using circles and arrows as shown at the top of this page.
5. In each circle write an "If...then" statement.
6. As the end is drawing near, remind the children that they will need to end in the same way they started. Example: The first circle says, "If you give a bunny a carrot, he's going to ask for lettuce. The last circle says, "If you give him a drink, he will want a carrot," which leads into the first circle again.
7. Invite children to use construction paper to create and cut out illustrations for the poem. Glue these onto the center of the poem.
8. Discuss what this circular book has added to your understanding of patterns. *(Possible answer: A pattern can be a story that repeats itself.)*

going further:

Read *Chicka Chicka Boom Boom* by Bill Martin, Jr. (Simon & Schuster, 1991), which also has a circular effect.

Animal Spots

Some of the most beautiful patterns are the overall patterns on the coats of animals. By creating spotted and striped animals, children will gain a deeper understanding of "overall" patterns.

Materials:

- *Animals* blacklines reproduced on tagboard
- yarn for tails
- books with illustrations or photos of African animals
- markers, scissors

Preparation:

- Gather books showing images of African wildlife from the library. For younger children, pre-cut the tagboard animal shapes.

Objectives:

- to help children understand an "overall pattern" in nature

Activity

1. Read *Bringing the Rain to Kapiti Plain* by Verna Aardema. Show the pictures, and ask what this book has to do with patterns. *(Animals' coats have a overall pattern.)*
2. Bring out the blacklines you reproduced on tagboard *(jaguar, giraffe, zebra)*. Let the children pick one of the tagboard animals, or distribute one to each child at random. Include two sets of "legs" with each animal body.
3. If you haven't already cut out the animal shapes, let the children do so.
4. Make books on wildlife available. Children can refer to these to determine the patterns and colors of their animals.
5. Have children use markers to decorate their animals with appropriate spots.
6. When the animals are complete, let children set up their creations on a display table.
7. Discuss some other animals with patterns *(Dalmatians, peacocks, cheetahs, etc.)*. Ask students to share what they have learned about patterns from this activity. *(Possible answer: Beautiful patterns appear in nature.)*

literature link:

Many animals with patterns on their coats are beautifully depicted in *Bringing the Rain to Kapiti Plain* by Verna Aardema *(Dial Books for Young Readers, 1981)*

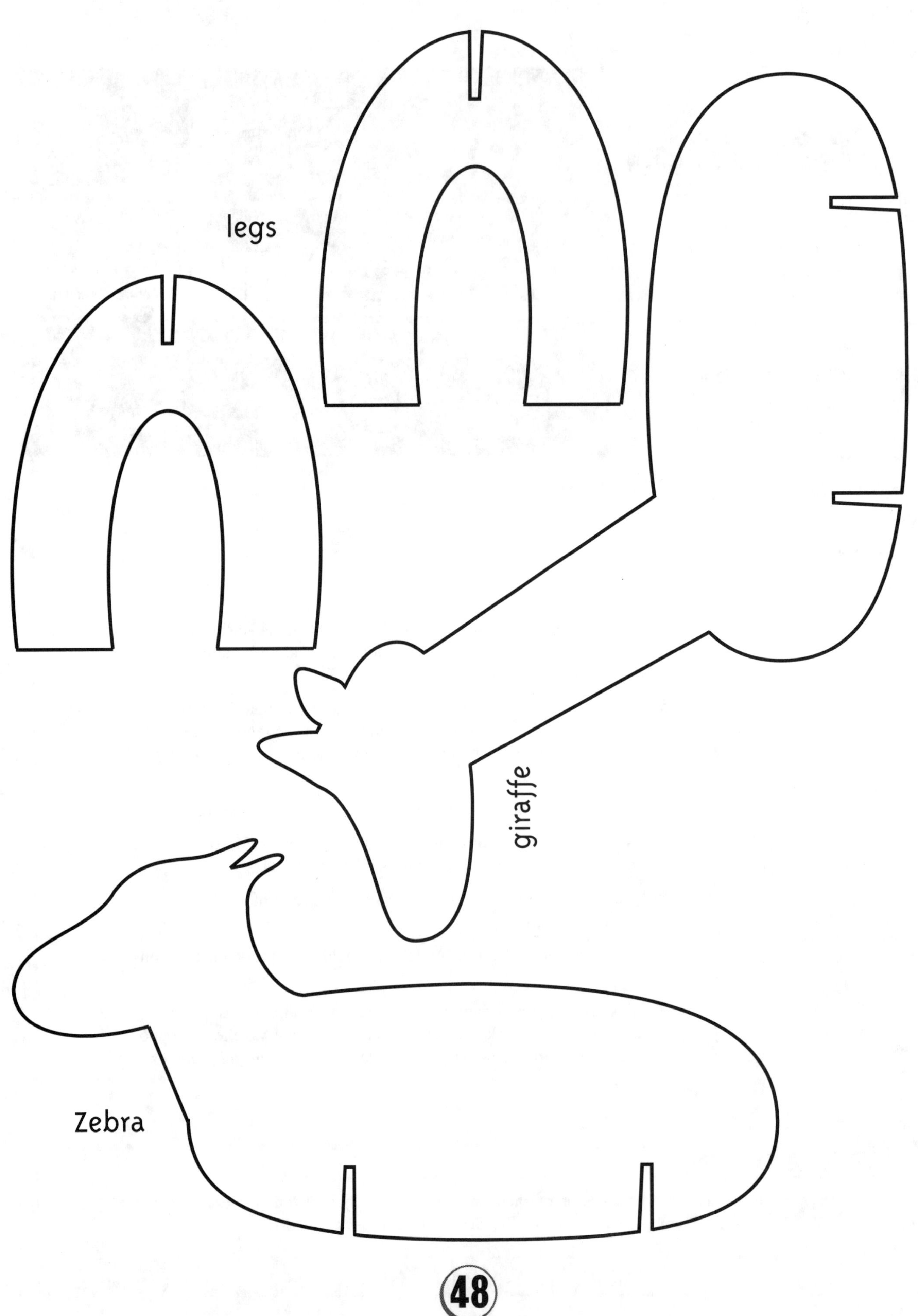
legs
giraffe
Zebra

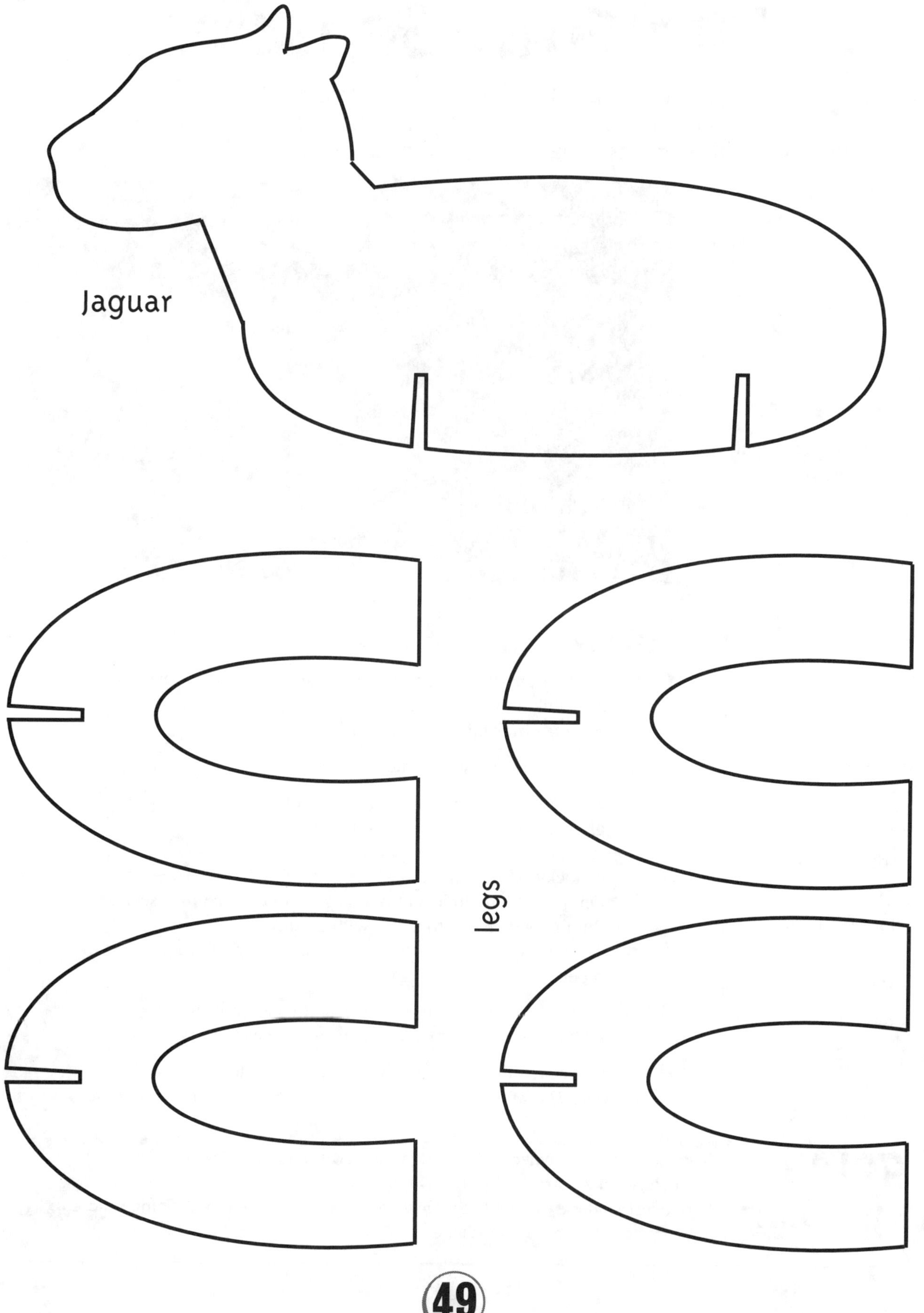
Jaguar
legs

The Four Seasons

Nature is full of cyclical patterns, from the four seasons to the life cycle of a frog. Here, children can build a model of a cyclical pattern that will help them visualize its repetitive, endless quality.

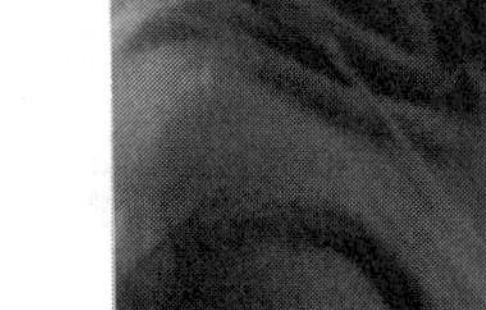

Objectives:

- to recognize cyclical patterns in nature
- to create a model of a cyclical pattern (the seasons)

Materials:

- 2 *Circle* blacklines per child (for younger children, pre-cut the circles)
- scissors
- brads
- markers or colored pencils
- books on the seasons

Activity

1. Explain that children will be making a spinner to show the four seasons. Talk about why the seasons are a pattern. *(They happen in the same order, year after year.)*
2. Model the steps of making the spinner:
   - **a.** Decorate each section of the first circle, drawing and labeling winter, spring, summer, and fall. Show the seasons in a clockwise direction.
   - **b.** On the second circle, cut out most of one of the four sections.
   - **c.** Put the two circles together with a brad.
   - **d.** Turn the spinner to show the endless pattern of seasons that repeats over and over again.
3. Distribute two *Circle* blacklines per child and help students follow the above steps to make their own "seasons" spinners.
4. As a class, review why the spinners show a pattern. *(Possible answer: The seasons repeat over and over again in the same order.)*

going further:

Brainstorm some other circular *(cyclical)* patterns in nature: day and night, the 4 stages of a butterfly *(egg to larva to pupa to butterfly)*, the 4 stages of a frog *(egg, tadpole, tadpole with back legs, frog)*, the 8 phases of the moon. Some children may want to make a second spinner.

Circle

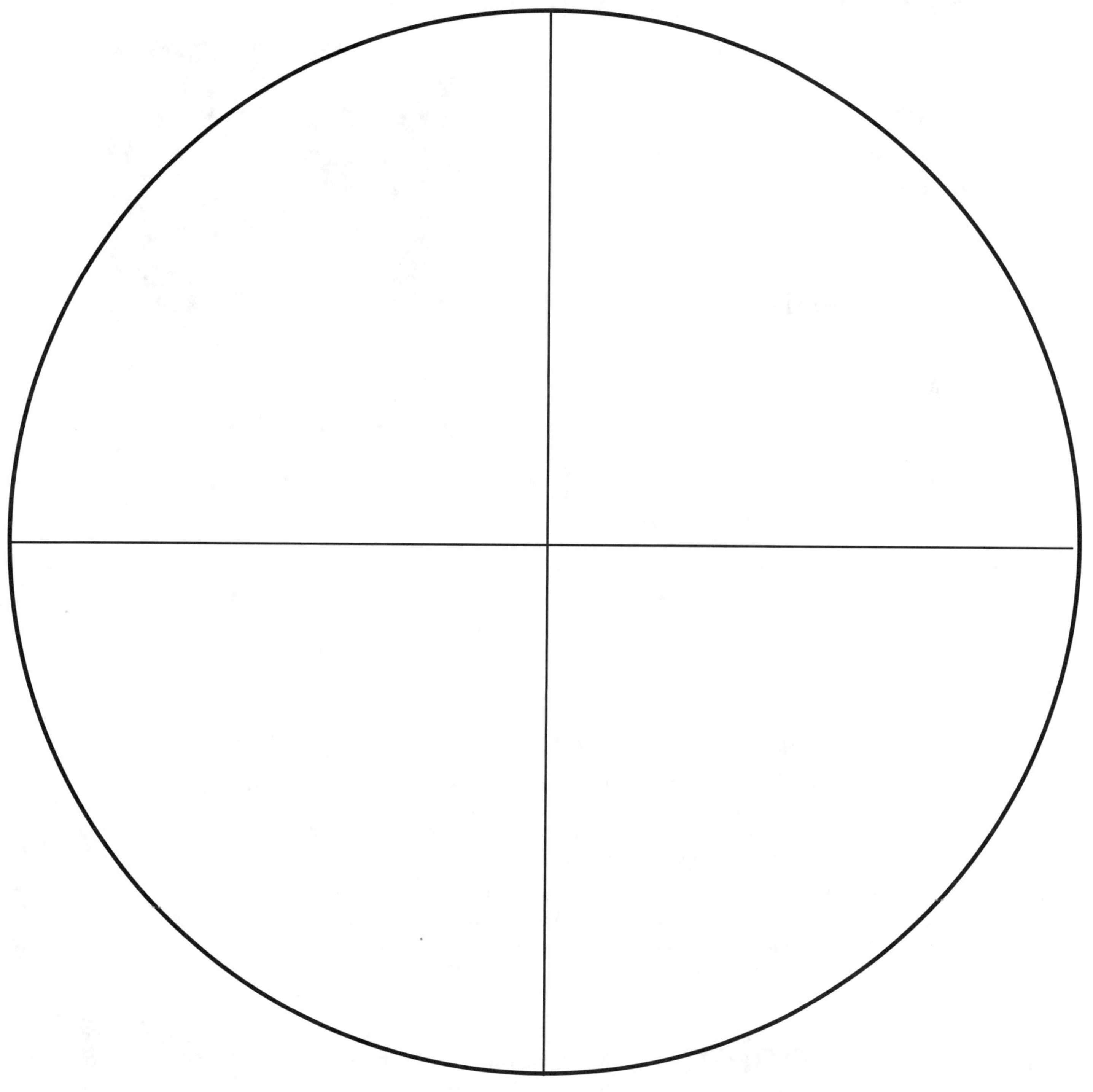

Beautiful **Butterfly**

Having children study pictures of real butterfly wings before they create their

Objectives:

- to complete and create symmetrical patterns
- to recognize a pattern in nature

Materials:

- books about butterflies
- *Pattern Block Butterfly* blackline
- Pattern Blocks
- glue and water mixture and paintbrush
- black construction paper
- construction paper scraps of many colors
- markers
- scissors

Activity

Variation 1: Pattern Block Butterflies

1. Ask children to describe butterflies they have seen. Then ask why the class might be making butterfly wings as part of a unit on patterns. *(Butterflies have a design on each wing that repeats on the other wing, making it a pattern.)*
2. Talk about symmetry and make a butterfly with your hands to reinforce the idea. Have children copy you. Ask, "Where are your pinkie fingers? Where are your pointer fingers?"

3. Show some real pictures of butterflies.
4. Pass out the Pattern Blocks and the *Pattern Block* blackline. Explain that children will be filling in the wings of the butterfly with a symmetrical pattern. Model the process using Pattern Blocks. See photo above.
5. Have children fill in one wing and then the other, making sure they are symmetrical. Another option is to have students work in pairs. One partner creates one wing and the other partner copies the pattern for the second wing.

If your students want to know more about butterflies, share these fascinating facts:

1. The wings are made of small scales that overlap each other like the shingles on a roof.

Wings

vn will help them appreciate and take notice of this amazing pattern in nature.

This butterfly is an example of a symmetrical pattern. It also incorporates a shrinking pattern, as the spots get smaller and smaller. The child picked the colors of the spots according to a rainbow pattern. She also used a pattern to determine the color of the small shape inside each spot.

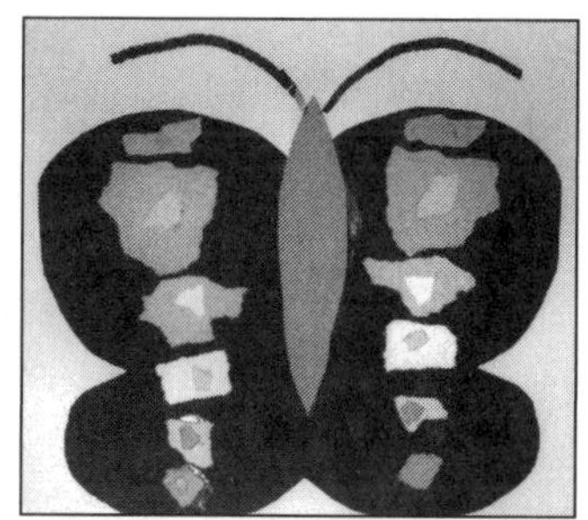

Activity

Variation 2: Cut Paper Butterflies

1. Let children design their own butterflies or have them work together in pairs, with each one responsible for making one of the symmetrical wings. First, students should fold a piece of black construction paper in half and draw the wings with pencil or chalk. Then they can cut along the pencil or chalk line through both layers of paper in order to cut out both wings at once.

2. Explain that children will be tearing pieces of construction paper to make colorful patterns on the wings. Model this process, emphasizing symmetry.

3. Some children may want to copy a real butterfly pattern. Some may also want to draw concentric circles that look like eyespots, like those found on real butterflies.

4. Have children glue down the torn shapes. Painting glue onto the whole wing (using a paintbrush) and sticking the shapes onto the glue is the easiest method.

5. The whole butterfly can be pasted to a piece of construction paper.

6. Antennae can be drawn or made from pipe cleaners.

2. Many animals like to eat butterflies. One of the butterfly's defenses is its ability to fly in a zig-zag pattern.

3. Butterfly wings look like leaves, making them good for camouflage.

4. Butterfly wings often have dots, called eyespots, that scare off animals who think the dots are the eyes of a large animal.

Pattern Block Butterfly

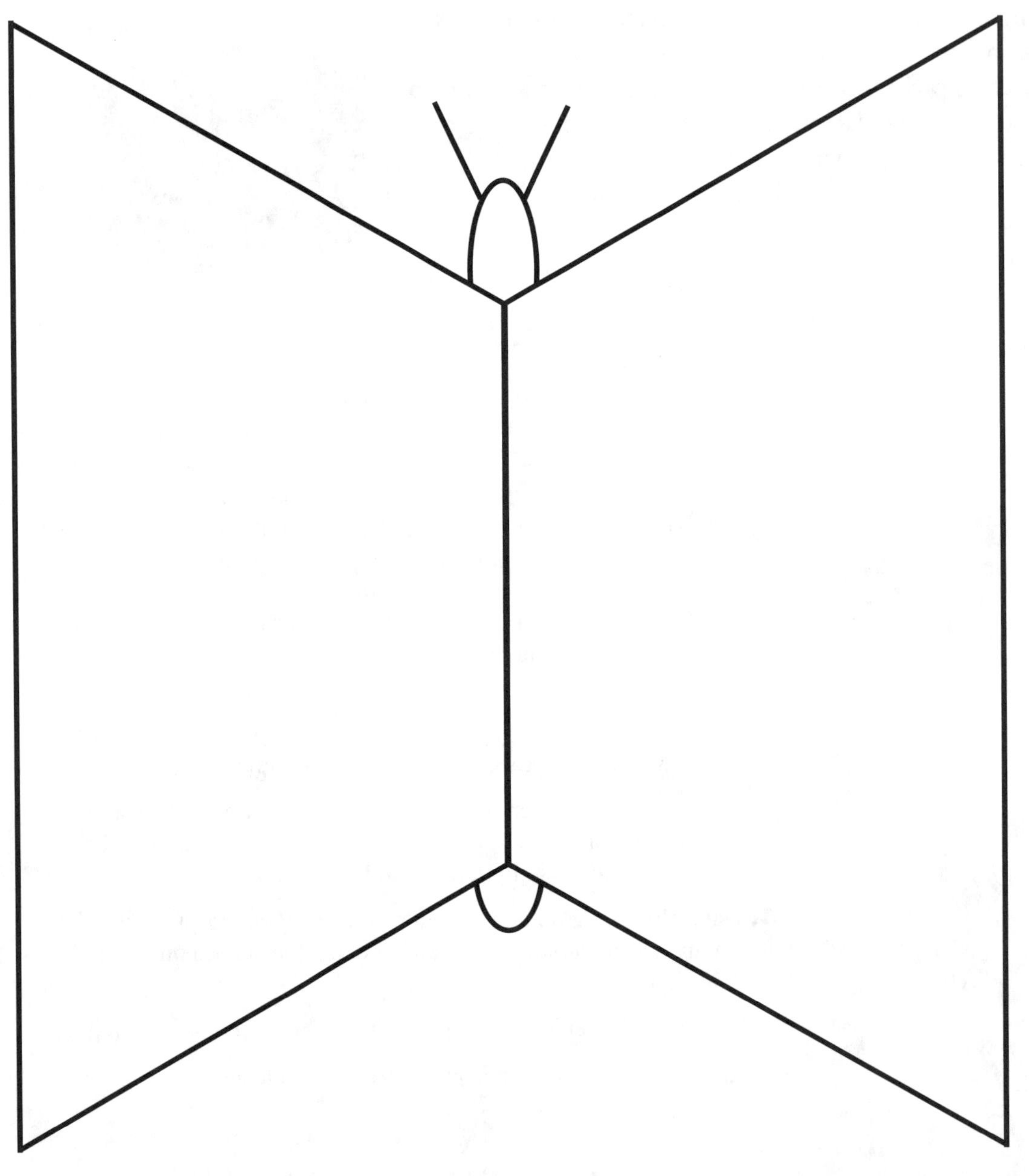

Snowflake Symmetry

Snowflakes offer numerous opportunities to explore symmetrical patterns.

Objective:

- to explore the symmetry of a six-sided snowflake crystal

Materials:

- square white paper 8 1/2" x 8 1/2" *(for younger children)*
- *Snowflake* blackline *(for older children)*
- hexagonal piece of waxed paper for use on the overhead *(optional)*
- *Snowflakes* by Joan Sugarman *(optional)* *(Little, Brown & Co., 1985)*

Preparation:

Before launching this activity, you may want to talk about snowflakes as a class. Some facts to introduce include:

- No two snowflakes are exactly alike
- Some snowflakes are six-sided plates
- Some snowflakes are six-sided crystals that look like stars

- As the starlike snowflakes fall from the clouds, they change shape. The farther they fall, the more complicated their designs become.

Activity

Variation 1: younger children

1. Pass out blank white squares and scissors. Have children fold their papers in half at least two times.

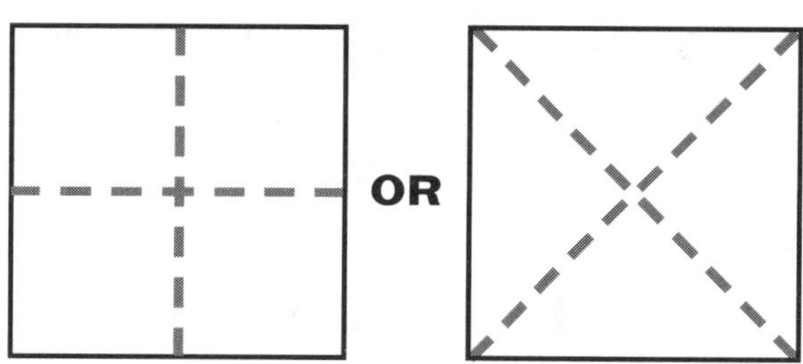

2. Invite children to cut the folded paper. Encourage them to cut at least one shape in each side and to vary the size of the shapes they cut.

3. Once snowflakes are opened up, let the children examine the pattern they have created. Ask if the snowflake has a pattern — a repeating part. Children may be able to identify a shape that repeats or a group of shapes that repeats.
4. Create a winter display.

Snowflake Symmetry

Variation 2: older children
Note: This variation involves more difficult folding and cutting.

1. Let older children create more scientifically accurate six-pointed snowflakes, using the *Snowflake* blackline.
2. Pass out the *Snowflake* blackline and scissors.
3. Ask children to cut out the hexagon on the blackline.
4. Have them fold the hexagon in half. If possible, model this with paper or with a waxed paper hexagon on the overhead. *(Folds show up well on the waxed paper.)*

5. Have children experiment. The goal is to fold the paper two more times and end up with 6 layers. A hint for the children: The final paper should look like an ice cream cone, or a triangle.

6. Have children fold the paper in half one more time.

7. Then the cutting can begin. Note that cutting out the upper right corner *(shown right)* results in starlike crystal shapes.

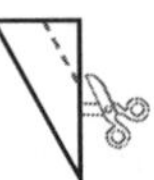

8. Have children find the repeating patterns on their opened snowflakes.
9. Display the snowflakes on a winter bulletin board.

Snowflake

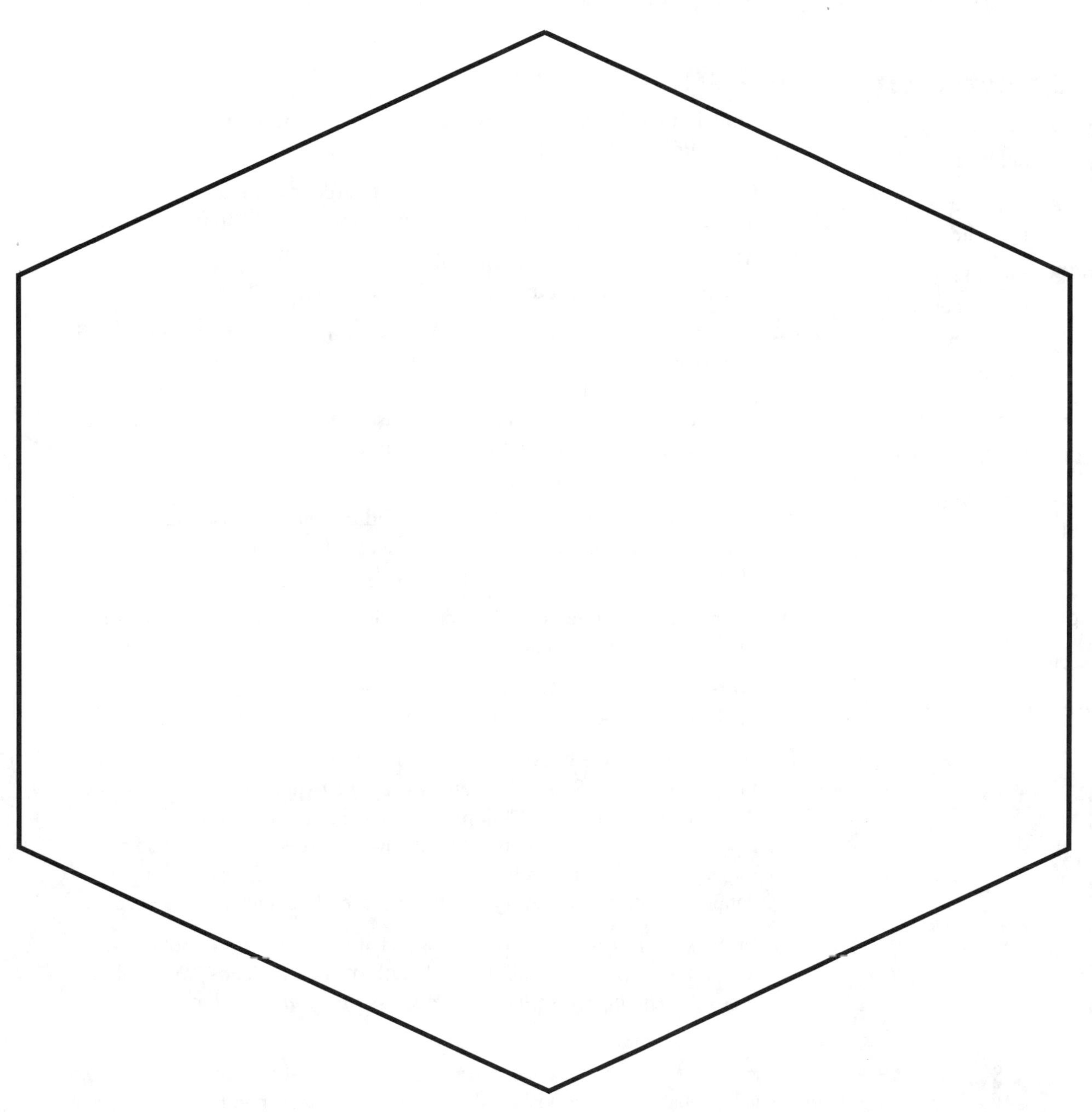

Sleeping Patterns of Animals

It is a scientist's job to collect data. Sometimes that data fits a general pattern. By looking at the sleeping habits of ten animals of varying sizes, children will discover an unexpected pattern.

Objectives:

- to organize and analyze data
- to make a hypothesis
- to find a pattern that is generally true

Materials:

- *Sleeping Animals* blackline
- markers
- pocket chart
- scissors

Activity

1. Explain that children will investigate how long different animals sleep. Point out that they will be looking for a pattern.
2. Pass out the *Sleeping Animals* blackline to groups of children. Have children cut the cards apart. Children may also wish to illustrate the cards.
3. As a class, discuss the various weights of the animals. Which is the heaviest animal? Which is the lightest?
4. Explain that the children will now be scientists. The question they will be investigating is: "Do you think the size of the animal has anything to do with how long it sleeps?" At first glance, the children may say there is no relationship because they assume that the question means, "Do you think that the larger an animal is, the longer it sleeps?"
5. After looking over the cards, some children may propose that the larger the animal, the fewer hours it sleeps. Or in a child's words, "How big they are, the less they sleep."
6. In groups, let children organize their cards to decide if the hypothesis is true. Some groups will arrange the cards by size, some by hours of sleep.
7. Work together to come to some conclusions. Begin by placing the cards on the classroom pocket chart in order of size or sleep times.
8. Ask children if the hypothesis seems to be true. Do larger animals seem to sleep less time. Some children will say the hypothesis is "mostly true." Ask if there is a pattern. Children may say that there is "sort of a pattern." This is an important point. Help children realize that sometimes in scientific research, there is "sort of a pattern," or most of the data fits a pattern. Not every animal or piece of data always fits exactly.
9. Probe students' understanding. Ask, "Think about a hippopotamus. What would you guess about the length of time it sleeps? What about a dog?" *(The hippo probably sleeps less time than the dog.)*

going further:

Students will probably want to know why some large animals need such little sleep. Scientists say that large plant-eating animals sleep for a short time because they spend so much of their day finding enough vegetation to feed themselves. (It takes a lot of leaves for a giraffe to feel full!)

Sleeping Animals

Anteater sleeps 12 hours weighs 75 pounds	**Elephant** sleeps 4 hours weighs 8,000 pounds
Chimp sleeps 10 hours weighs 110 pounds	**Squirrel** sleeps 14 hours weighs 3 pounds
Cow sleeps 7 hours weighs 900 pounds	**Cat** sleeps 13 hours weighs 12 pounds
Jaguar sleeps 11 hours weighs 150 pounds	**Dolphin** sleeps 5 hours weighs 440 pounds

Hand Band

Using their hands as rhythm instruments is natural for children and can help them get a real feel for sound patterns.

Objectives:

- to create rhythmic sound patterns with hands or rhythm sticks
- to describe sound patterns in words

Materials:

- ▲ rhythm sticks or blocks *(both optional)*

Activity

1. Seat children in a circle. Explain that children will be forming a band, using a natural percussion instrument — their hands.
2. Model some easy ways to make sounds with your hands: claps, snaps, slapping your knees, and slapping the floor. When students have tried each sound, experiment with some rhythms. Say the pattern in words: "Knees, clap, floor, floor."
3. To help students follow a longer rhythmic pattern, draw symbols or write words ("clap," "snap," etc.) on pocket chart cards and display the cards in the desired order.
4. Have children take turns thinking of a rhythmic pattern for everyone to copy. The student who came up with the pattern can be the one to call out the sequence for others to follow.
5. You can also divide children into pairs and have them make up rhythmic patterns such as the following: legs, legs, clap, clap, partner clap, partner clap, partner clap.
6. Discuss what was special about this pattern activity and what students learned. *(Possible answers: We used our own bodies to make patterns. The whole class followed the same pattern at the same time.)*

literature link:

Read *Over in the Meadow* by Olive A. Wadsworth (Four Winds Press, 1971). Make a rhythmic series of claps to go with the book.

Water Music

Music is all about patterns. The notes on a scale create a pattern for the ears. Children can recreate this pattern by making their own instrument.

Objectives:

- to recognize growing and shrinking patterns
- to hear and create musical patterns

Materials:

- ▲ 8 glasses or glass pop bottles
- ▲ a plastic pitcher of water
- ▲ spoon to play the instrument

Preparation:

- ▲ Create 8 small cards with a circle of a different color on each one, representing the notes of the scale *(C D E F G A B C)*
- ▲ Make pocket chart strips with music written on them in the form of colored circles *(see page 62 for some simple tunes to try)*.

Activity

1. To create the instrument, fill the glasses to different levels, starting with a glass that's almost full and ending with a glass that has just a little bit of water. Test the scale and adjust the water if necessary. *(The less water, the higher the note.)*
2. Demonstrate by tapping the spoon on the edge of each glass, going from most full to least full. Ask children to describe the pattern. Some will say the water level gets lower and lower. Others will say the notes grow higher.
3. Ask children to describe the relationship between water level and how high or low the note is.
4. Place the cards of different colors in front of the glasses.
5. Place a song strip in front of the glasses.

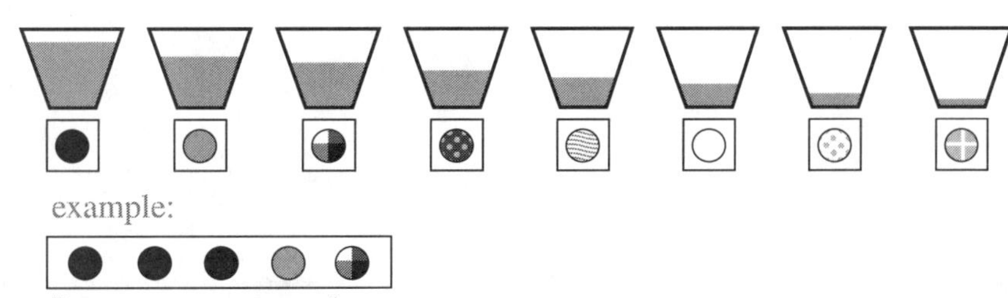

example:

Row, row, row your boat

6. Let children take turns playing parts of tunes on the instrument. Use tunes from page 62 or tunes they make up.
7. Discuss what students learned about patterns from experimenting with "water music." *(Possible responses: Some patterns are heard instead of seen. When we play music, we are creating a pattern for someone to repeat.)* The notes of the scale form a pattern.

Tunes to Try

Reproduce these tunes on pocket chart strips or pieces of construction paper. Use the eight colors your class has decided upon to represent the notes. *(We have used numbers since the page is not in color.)*

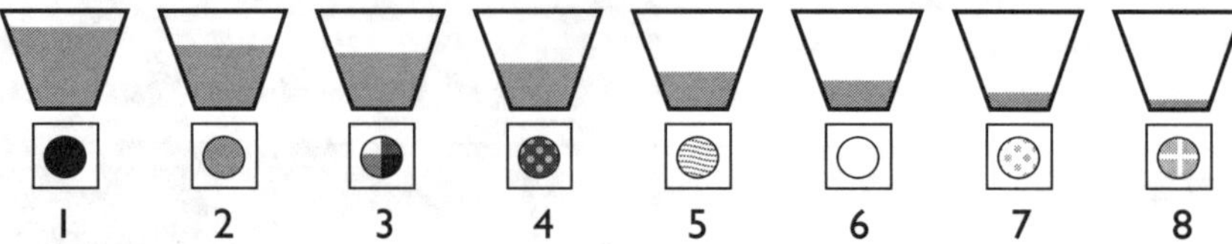

Row, Row, Row Your Boat

1 1 1 2 3 3 2 3 4 5 8 8 8 5 5 5 3 3 3 1 1 1 5 4 3 2 1

Twinkle, Twinkle, Little Star

Rock-a-Bye, Baby

Pattern Party

To wrap up a unit on patterns, why not throw a party? Children can decorate the room with their favorite pattern projects and use their woven mats for place mats. For party favors, children can make patterned bookmarks. During the party, read the pattern-filled tale *The Fat Cat* by Jack Kent. Kids can decorate "fat cat" cookies with candy placed in a pattern. You can even invite another class!

Materials:

- ▲ blank papers for children to write what they have learned about patterns
- ▲ materials for making bookmarks: tagboard cut into cat shapes, stickers, stars, markers, ribbon for tail, stamps and stamp pads, tape or paste

Activity

PART I: PREPARING FOR THE PARTY AND MAKING BOOKMARKS

1. Explain that the class will be throwing a pattern party.
2. Make the bookmarks that will be used for party favors:
   - Show a tagboard cat with a ribbon for its tail.
   - Show the materials available for making the bookmark. Let children help plan what the bookmarks will look like.
   - Explain that the bookmarks will be made on an assemblyline. Discuss what an assemblyline is and how it involves a pattern.
   - Have several assemblylines running at once, so that all children can take part.
   - Divide up the tasks on the assemblyline so that each child or pair of children have a task they do over and over again. Examples: cutting out the ears; drawing nose, mouth, and whiskers; drawing eyes; putting on stickers; taping or pasting on tails, writing words on it.
3. Decorate the room with past pattern projects.
4. Brainstorm what the class has learned about patterns and keep a record on chart paper. Hand out blank papers for children to write one special thing they have learned about patterns. Use these for a bulletin board.

Pattern Party

Objectives:

- to display and share pattern work
- to summarize what children have learned about patterns
- to recognize the pattern in a cumulative story

Materials:

- *The Fat Cat* by Jack Kent (Scholastic, 1971)
- laminated woven placemats set out on tables/desks *(from page 39)*
- baked sugar cookies in the shape of "fat cats" with icing already on them, raisins and candies for decorating the cookies
- completed bookmarks

Activity

Part 2: PARTY STORYTIME AND SNACKS

1. Read the story *The Fat Cat* and let children predict the cumulative pattern on each page.
2. Let the children decorate the iced cat cookies in patterns using different candies.
3. Pass out the bookmarks as party favors.
4. Other possible party activities include:
   - Do a clapping activity in a circle, where one child starts and everyone copies.
   - Play "water music" using the instructions from page 61.

variation: Substitute *The Gingerbread Boy* by Richard Egielski (HarperCollins, 1997) for *The Fat Cat*. Then children can make gingerbread man cookies. Note that this story has a different kind of pattern – the Gingerbread Man says the same refrain over and over again.